# "Shining Stars"

Inspiring Stories and Simple Steps to Empower
You to Achieve Your Highest Potential

*Produced by:*

# Teresa Hailey

*Denver, Colorado*

www.trafford.com
North America & international
toll-free: 1 888 232 4444 (USA & Canada)
fax: 812 355 4082

# Dedication

I dedicate this book to **Dr. Mary McLeod Bethune** (1875–1955) who was the most outstanding international leader of black women from the 1920s to the 1950s. Dr. Mary McLeod Bethune died at the age of seventy-nine. She is buried on the grounds of Bethune-Cookman College which continues to educate many of the nation's African American leaders (nwhm.org).

Education is and has always been very important to me. In 2012, I decided to go back to college after being out for some thirty years. I noticed that I was having a very hard time learning, so I went to four different doctors who all told me that I would not be able to learn and earn a college degree. I was told that I have a learning disorder. I was also told to apply for Social Security disability because I would not be able to work. I stand holding my head very high, proud to announce that I earned my second college degree in December 2014 from Colorado Technical University, Aurora, Colorado. I'm a living witness what prayer and hard work can do. I say to any parent, if a doctor tells you or your child you cannot learn, *you need to find a way.* For example, in 2013, I needed to pass basic math for my degree. After four attempts, summer school, help from a tutor, I passed the class. If one way does not work, you have to keep trying. *Never* give up. I now understand that I learn by blocks, charts, flash cards. At times I even need someone to read to me.

It's because of Dr. Bethune's dedication to education I ride on her shoulders. She paved the way for my success. Dr. Mary McLeod Bethune was a revolutionary educator who not only provided her students with an academic education but also with an education in life. She gave them the skills and confidence necessary to be successful, and she set standards for today's historic black colleges. An educator not merely for her students but for the entire world.

When Dr. Bethune was twenty-nine years old, she opened the Daytona Beach Literary and Industrial School for Training Negro Girls. In 1929, the school was renamed Bethune-Cookman College; it ended its high school program in 1936 and issued its first college degrees in 1943. Dr. Bethune served as president even as she became increasingly a national and international figure (nwhm.org).

During World War I, she encouraged African Americans to participate in the Red Cross. In 1920, after women gained the vote, she led black women in using their new right. Perhaps more than any other person, she was key to the transition of blacks from the Republican Party—"the party of Lincoln"—to the Democratic Party and its New Deal during the Great Depression. Dr. Bethune became a close friend of Eleanor Roosevelt, and in 1936, Franklin Roosevelt appointed her as head of the National Youth Administration, a vocational education program aimed at minorities. For years into the future, this would remain the highest governmental position held by a black woman. She also served on the advisory board that created the Women's Army Corps, and she saw that the corps was racially integrated from its 1942 beginning (nwhm.org).

In 1931, when racism remained routine, she was so obviously meritorious that Dr. Bethune ranked tenth on a journalists' list of America's most outstanding women. Her most important achievement arguably was the one that gave her an international audience when President Harry Truman appointed her to the 1945 Founding Conference of the United Nations. No African nation or any other nation sent a black female delegate, and Dr. Mary McLeod Bethune represented all the world's women of color. In 1949, she probably was the **first black woman granted an honorary degree by a college** for white women; Orlando's Rollins College, a rather elite institution, awarded it six years prior to her death. Among many other honors, the U.S. Post Office recognized Dr. Bethune by issuing a first-class stamp with her image in 1985.

Dr. Bethune was also a businesswoman. She invested in real estate, owned one fourth of a resort in Daytona, and was a founder of an insurance company. By 1952, all the men who cofounded Central Life Insurance Company of Tampa with her in 1923 had died, and Dr. Bethune became president. At that time, she was the only woman in America, white or black, to hold this position (nwhm.org).

I'm sad that I never had an opportunity to meet Dr. Mary McLeod Bethune. It gives me great pride and honor to introduce her granddaughter to you, Dr. Evelyn Bethune whose chapter will be the first that you will read.

# References:

Flemming, Sheila, Retrieved January 1, 2015, www.nwhm. org/education-resource, National Women's History Museum, Education and Resources, Dr. Mary McLeod Bethune 1875–1955, Biography

# Contents

# Acknowledgments

*I* want to first thank God and give him all the glory and praise for blessing me with an opportunity to do this book project. Second, I want to take this opportunity to thank my parents George and Mary Hailey. Who afforded me the opportunity to be born and raised in a very loving two-parent home. They provided me with the things that I needed and wanted. To the both of you, I will always be grateful.

To the man who paid for this book to be published, and requested anonymity, what can I say? You are truly the greatest and an angel sent from above. I often think, *God, why me*? You could have selected anyone to be a blessing to others. You have changed my life; your wisdom, knowledge, grace and leadership will always be with me. I thank you and your wife for allowing me to attend your corporate board room meetings and meetings with bank officials requesting millions of dollars really opened my eyes to the business world. Thank you for selecting me to be a part of your millionaire club mentorship program, for trusting me with your customized one-of-a-kind Rolls Royce and for allowing me to be a part of your family. You believe in me, and in my potential.

To my godmother, Ms. Hartene Britt, who has been in my life for some forty-plus years, you are a woman of God. I thank you for your daily prayers, love, and understanding. Thank you for always handling all situations with grace and dignity. "You are my queen."

To Mrs. Paula R. Bryant, whom I have had the honor and pleasure of knowing for some thirty years. I remember when we met in Junior high School, I knew you were special, and knowing you as an adult, you are an angel sent from above. You mean the world to me.

To Dr. Shirley Clark, I will always appreciate your wisdom, expertise, and knowledge. Thank you for guiding me through this book process. You are a winner.

To my "Shining Stars" Executive Committee, Mrs. Paula R. Bryant and Dr. Stan (Breakthrough) Harris I appreciate your knowledge and wisdom. To my co-authors:

| | |
|---|---|
| Dr. Evelyn Bethune | Ms. Sarah Bryant |
| Dr. Stan (Breakthrough) Harris | Mrs. Paula R. Bryant |
| Mr. Joshua Schular | Ms. Katrina Ferguson |
| Mr. Harold J. Parker, MBA | Dr. Jamal Rasheed |
| Dr. Shirley Clark | Staff Sgt. Joshua Harris |
| Mr. Hasaan Rasheed, M.Ed. | |

You gave your time and talents to write a chapter in this book, which brought a lot of class, credibility and dignity. To my relatives, family and friends, I will always be grateful for your love, prayers, and support.

Teresa Hailey, Producer
"Shining Stars"

# Foreword

*I* write this foreword with respect and sincerity for this collaborative effort that each contributor selected has a life journey that, when shared herein, can give the reader perspective, encouragement, and an appreciation for the overwhelming joy of just living—all this despite the difficulties, challenges, and even sadness, one endures along the way.

In my life experience as an international traveler and educator, I have come to believe that human beings tend to overweigh the negative and underappreciate the positive in their lives, supported by our various media sources. This work will help counteract this contention.

At the winter of my life, I now understand, as do these contributors, that for every sad, weak, or poor experience in our lives and in every nation and organization, there are one hundred good, positive, and valuable experiences at the same time. I hope you feel this with each piece in this work.

Lloyd S. Lewan, EdD, LHD, LLD
Lewan and Associates
Denver, Colorado

# Introduction

About twenty years ago I was the State Director for the Teen, Miss, and Ms. Black Colorado Pageant, I was invited to the home of one of Colorado's millionaires for a Christmas party. We instantly became friends. He sponsored one of my pageants, and has always been very supportive of me. He believes in giving back, and servicing as mentors to others that are determined to be successful. One day I was visiting him and his wife at their home in the mountains (of Colorado) I was talking about how important it is to have a Living Will and a life insurance policy. Many families today are not speaking to each other after the death of a love one. A illness can divide a family. I was talking about the death of my mother, he got up and walked out of the room, I was first very upset, because I was talking and he just left me talking. He later returned, and handed me a check for thousands of dollars, and told me to go write my book. He had one big requested, I could not release his name, and he wanted to remain anonymous. He later explained how, he and his brother had not spoken in over ten years after the death of their mother. He stated that it is very important to inform people just how important having a Living Will and a life insurance policy is.

The money sat in my savings account for about six months, while I researched every publishing company. After many hours of praying and asking God for direction, I selected a publishing company. I look at my gift as being a blessing from God. I often hear, "if you help someone get what they want, God will help you get what you want." I wanted to make people authors who had never been, and I wanted each author to make over $100,000.00 from the book.

I first wanted to write my own book after being blessed with the opportunity to work and travel with Rev. Hosea Williams who was a Field General for Dr. Martin Luther King, Jr. I met Rev. Williams why'll working on Rev. Jesse Jackson Presidential campaign. One day a group of us was registering and educating people to vote who lived in rural areas of Georgia. After being in the hot sun, walking, and talking to people all day we were all tired and ready to go home. When we returned back to our van, we were met by five Ku Klux Klan members dressed in full Klan regalia. Because of my fast thinking and determination to stand-up; I was able to get us out of a very dangerous situation unharmed. For days it was the talk around the office. Word got back to Rev. Williams who invited me to work and travel with him. I was traveling with Rev. Williams's every day, anywhere from two to five people would always stop him asking for assistance. Rev. Williams was very well known in the community. Regardless, if they had been fired from their job, facing jail time, or experiencing discrimination, etc., I would help assist in gathering information. Rev. Williams would then investigate and determined which direction to go. My most rewarding experience working with Rev. Williams came when myself and a few others were successful at getting him.

Williams re-elected for State Representative while he was in jail. While organizing a march in Forsyth, Georgia where we were invited by a citizen of Forsyth to attend a Martin Luther King, March. We were met by a group of Caucasian people throwing bottles, calling us names, and letting us know that we were not welcome there. Later, I learned that not one Black or minority person lived there. Within ten days, Rev. Williams had contacted national leaders all over the U.S. and took thousands of people back to Forsyth, Georgia for a March and rally. I remember that there was so many marchers we all could not fit in the city.

When I first started writing my life story, something was missing. I was not happy; I wanted more. I wanted and needed for this book to be a blessing for others. So I made it into a collaborative book. I wanted the book to be able to inspire and motivate others to reach and achieve their highest potential. I wanted each author, and nonprofit organizations that I support to attain a financial blessing from this book. And I wanted to give money to a person that lost his or her business to the rioting and fires in Ferguson, Missouri. The rioting took place after the police killing of a young African American boy. We as a nation have come a long way, yet racism and discrimination are very much alive. I am also going to give a portion of my royalties to my high school (Thomas Jefferson High School/Denver, Colorado) to start the Paula R. Bryant scholarship foundation.

There are still cities where blacks and other minorities cannot live. There are still Fortune 500 companies who refuse to promote blacks and minorities to management, executive positions, or board members. In 2015, minorities are still the last hired and the first fired.

We are living in a give me, I want and I need generation. A generation that wants everything now handed to them. Learning communication skills and planning for the future is not a part of their life. A generation where too many parents spoil and allow their children to talk back, be disrespectful and do as they please. Parents set no boundaries or standards for their children.

I wanted to show others that regardless of what hand life deals you, you can still rise above it. You can still have the American dream. Develop your plan, and then apply it. Turning to drugs, alcohol and suicide is not the answer.

*Part 1*

# God, Family, and Education

Dr. Evelyn Bethune

"For God so loved the world, that he gave his only begotten son, that whosoever believeth in him should not perish, but have everlasting life" (Saint John 3:16, King James Version).

# The Journey

*Dr. Evelyn Bethune*

*"I*f I had known that it would be this hard, I might not have done it." Those were the words of a student that I mentor as she was venting about the difficulties of college life. As she was speaking, my mind began to drift into memory lane. Those words could have been my own not too long ago and on certain days, may still drift through the shadows of my mind. As I half-listened, half-remembered, I heard my mother say, "Just wait until you get to be my age."

Now here I am, my mother's age at the time she spoke those words, with a much clearer understanding of *The Journey*. As I brought myself back into full focus with my young mentee, I knew that the next words I said to her held great value, as she was looking for a reason to move forward . . . even though her words, and maybe even her mind, were trying to find a reason to quit. In a quiet, calm voice, I began to tell her about another young woman whom many would have said would not amount to much of anything. Her circumstances would dictate that she would probably spend her life uneducated, poor, and relegated to the lower rungs of what life had to offer. Yet in spite of the obstacles of poverty, segregation, parents who were newly freed slaves now sharecroppers, and no visible possibilities for an education, this young woman became an advisor to four United States presidents over her lifetime. She founded a school, which is now a university, and changed the very direction of American history. The value that she added to this country and the world cannot be measured, and it affected the lives of millions of people.

The impact made by Dr. Mary Jane McLeod Bethune is a part of the very fabric of our country. *The Journey* for her started in July 1875 on a sharecropper's farm in South Carolina and ended May 1955 on the campus of Bethune-Cookman College, which she founded in 1904 in Daytona

Beach, Florida. If Dr. Bethune had known that *it would be as hard as it was*, she might not have done it . . . but she did. She might not have taken the first step or may have chosen a different route. We are all on a journey, and depending on which road we choose, we will either progress or digress. I explained to my mentee that the decision to attend college is a big one, but staying and completing what you start, with excellence, is an even greater challenge. Give up, fail, or press on, complete your task and succeed. Which road will you choose? I am glad that she chose to stay. She will graduate in May 2015. *The Journey* continues.

Somewhere along the way we discover that as much as we might think that we are in control of *The Journey*, once we start on a particular path, changing direction can be both energizing and euphoric yet quite challenging. Many times, especially when we are young and full of ourselves, we start out thinking that the world owes us something (when it doesn't) and that we are "all that and a bag of chips" only to discover that there is nothing new under the sun. There may be new technology and a new name, but the situations remain the same. The lessons to be learned are the same today as yesterday and tomorrow. These are the lessons that we will value the most: learning respect, the difference between knowledge and wisdom, the value of remembering the past and building on it, patience, kindness, compassion, endurance, enjoying learning are all steps along the journey.

There was a time in the African American community when education was a valued commodity, and those who provided it were a respected part of the community. Teachers were placed in the same category as doctors and lawyers and even pastors. They were anchors in the community and worked as a team with parents to create learning environments that nurtured young minds to develop into the best minds that they could be. For the most part, the thought of disrespecting a teacher would never enter the mind of a student without the immediate thought of consequences from a parent. Teachers were treasured because of the value they added to the quality of life of a community. For many of us, they were the examples for how to walk, talk, dress, and just "be." It was never difficult to distinguish between teacher and student. Striving for excellence was the norm and not the exception. Throughout the segregated south, it was understood that you had to be twice as good as "other folks" to rise to the top. So that was *The Journey* . . . to be twice as good.

My journey began at 605½ Second Avenue. We lived there until 1968 when "urban renewal" came to Daytona and destroyed our neighborhood in the name of progress. Our house and my oldest brother's house were next door to each other, and there was a barbecue stand in the front yard that was run by Mr. Pinkston and his family. Our yard was big enough to play tag football, and we had plenty of space for hide-and-seek. Across the street was Allen Chapel AME Church and Mr. Glover's photoshop. On the same side of the street as the photoshop was Gainous Funeral Home, and on the second floor of *that* building was Dr. Brunson's dental office and the apartment where Cousin Lucille lived. Cousin Lucille was Mother Dear's niece. We could look out of our back door at the college campus. The road that separated our house from the college was tagged the Gym Road because Moore's Gymnasium was located on the other side. When school was closed for Christmas, the campus of Bethune-Cookman served as the neighborhood gathering place because the sidewalks and open fields were the best in the neighborhood for nonstop skating, bike riding, and just hanging out with friends.

On the Fourth of July, we could sit on our fence and watch the fireworks that were soaring in the air from the beach. I used to wonder why we never went to the beach in Daytona to watch until I got older and realized that black people in Daytona were not allowed on the beach after 5:00 p.m. unless they were working. We could not get in the ocean in Daytona, the worlds' most famous beach. That was a WOW (With-Out Words) moment for me.

Most of the children in our neighborhood went to the same nursery, Sara Hunts Nursery School, the same elementary school, Bonner Elementary, and went to the same high school, Campbell Junior and Senior High. If we were lucky, we got to leave Daytona to go to college; but if not, we could go to the mighty Bethune-Cookman College or the Volusia County Vocational School.

Attending Sara Hunt's Nursery School meant that you got the best start you possibly could for an education. Behind the building that housed the nursery and pre-K classes was the Sara Hunt Orphanage. This was the place where the children who had no family were taken care of. My mom was a beautician, so we spent some Saturdays at the orphanage while our mother and members of the Beauty Culture Organization did the hair of the little girls at the orphanage. As children, we *adopted* these children who became like our brothers and sisters. We made sure that we remembered birthdays and special holidays with gifts and outings. Our mother was one of the most dynamic women that you would ever meet. First, she was drop-dead gorgeous. Second, she was incredibly smart and creative. She was also filled with a desire to make the world a better place, and she gave that sensibility to her children. *The Journey* is filled with people to keep and ones to love, from afar as well as some people to discard completely. This is what shapes our experiences. Our abilities to make decisions and the right choices are all based on how we process the information that we are given and our perceptions of the situations we encounter along the way. The people in our circle help us to define those experiences based on how they respond or explain our encounters. Parents and teachers are critical to the shaping of perceptions and our understanding of situations because most of our time is spent with these people in particular during our early years. They are our examples of good and evil.

For example, there was another side to our mother. There was that side of her that said to us "Wherever you embarrass me is where I am going to embarrass you." We did not test this very often because we knew that she meant it. I have often said that in our household, Mommy was the crucifixion and Daddy was grace and mercy. They were consistent in their roles as parents, setting guidelines, and parameters. We knew who was in charge, and it wasn't us. Our parents taught us respect for authority and demanded excellence in how we behaved and the work we did, whether in school or out.

Now if I never talk about anything else, I have to talk about Bonner Elementary. The school was located across from Pine Haven Projects and, like everything else on our side of the tracks, was in need of everything, except good teachers. You see, we had the best already.

When I first arrived at Bonner, Mrs. Evelyn Bonner was our principal. I loved that she had the same first name as me. She retired the following year, and Mrs. LaRosa Smith became our principal. She always had a smile for us. The beauty of it all was that they lived in the same neighborhood as we did, so we saw them all the time. Even after leaving a certain grade, the next year we always went back to visit our previous teachers because we loved them so much. Mrs. Rose Marie Bryant taught us Bible verses and how to be human beings instead of heathens, and it worked for most of us. I would say that most of the poetry that I have committed to heart was taught to me by Mrs. Willie Ruth Jones at Bonner Elementary. These teachers also taught us to love the arts and the humanities, reading, and performance arts, such as the ballet and the symphony.

In 1958, as a first grade, I was elected Little Miss Bonner Elementary. This was the year they changed the name of the elementary school from Cypress Street Elementary to honor Mrs. Evelyn Bonner. I really think I got elected because my niece Patricia got all her friends to vote for me. I loved school, especially Bonner. They taught with old books and fewer supplies than the teachers at white schools, but they gave so much to us that we did not know we were working with less. They told us that if we could read the old books, we could read the new ones. By the time I was in second grade, I was reciting "The Creation" by James Weldon Johnson, and I did it so well that the principal, Mrs. LaRosa Smith, took me to other schools to show off my skills.

There were always opportunities for the children to stand up in front of people and recite what we had learned. Most importantly, there was an environment that nurtured us and teachers who made us feel like we could achieve anything that we set our minds to. These teachers taught us to love learning and to embrace it and that it took discipline to achieve excellence. They taught with passion, discipline, and an expectation of excellence. Even the cafeteria workers took great care of us. Mrs. Newkirk made sure that no child went hungry, and Mrs. Anderson could fix fish and spinach so good that you wanted to eat your vegetables. Right today, I love spinach cooked with boiled eggs in it because that was how I learned to eat it at Bonner Elementary.

It was in the sixth grade, in Mrs. Gainous's class, that I learned of the assassination of John F. Kennedy. I remember Mrs. Gainous being called out of our class and coming back in tears. We were afraid. When she told us that the president of the United States had been assassinated, we were in shock, and we all began to cry. It was her reassurances that helped us work through what we were feeling. We were old enough and smart enough to know that this was not a good thing.

It was at Bonner Elementary that we learned how to walk up- and downstairs and how to enter a room. We also learned to get underneath our desks in case of an invasion or the dropping of bombs. We had evacuation drills to get us ready because during this time, the USA was dealing with the Bay of Pigs and Batista being kicked out of Cuba. He sought political asylum and moved to Miami, so we had to be ready just in case that little island, ninety miles off the coast of Miami, decided to attack us. Now here we are today repairing our relationship with Cuba because of President Obama. *The Journey* continues . . .

In 1965, we came to a fork in the road called integration, and we took the path that seemed most popular. This path led to access and not ownership, and though it appeared that we were moving forward, time has made us rethink our position and reevaluate whether or not, in actuality, we have moved at all. In the areas of education, we did not think about what we were giving up in the process: the best of ourselves.

There was something much worse than the Cuban Missile Crisis that occurred during this time. It was called freedom of choice, and this portion of *The Journey* really caused a rift in the world of many black children. Wikipedia states, "*Freedom of Choice (free transfer also)* was the name for a number of plans developed in the United States during 1965–1970, aimed at the integration of schools in states that had a segregated educational system." Instead of just letting us go to the traditional junior high school, some of our parents got together and decided that because of the opportunity provided by freedom of choice, now was the time to integrate/desegregate the schools in Daytona Beach.

Our parents, with the guidance of some school administrators, decided that they would send the top students from the black elementary and junior high schools to ensure that we were able to handle the work. We were placed in white junior high and high schools in the hopes that there could be a quiet change instead of forced compliance. While the schoolwork was easy, it was the acts of physical assault, such as being spit on in the hallway on your way to class or being pushed down a flight of stairs or shoved into a locker for which we were not prepared. We were not prepared for the open hostility of most of the teachers, administrators, parents, and of course, our fellow students. Other than the janitor, there were no black people but us on campus. There was nothing that a black child could do or say in defense of their actions that was not twisted into a suspension for the black child. It didn't matter that you may have been defending yourself. With few exceptions and little help, we were treated with hostility, and we knew we were not wanted there.

I was always grateful that every day, when I came out of that building, my daddy was there to pick me up. I did not have to walk home like many of my classmates, and I did not have to be afraid that someone would pick a fight once they left the school grounds. Anger was a big part of our lives back then because we had no voice, and we felt the hot sting of racism without being equipped to deal with it. Many times we wondered out loud why our parents would send us to such an awful place. As children, we could not understand why they thought we would get a better education in a place where we were not wanted and taught by teachers who, for the most part, did not want to teach us. Many of my fellow black classmates carried the scars, mental and physical, of our time at Mainland Junior High and "freedom of choice."

We were still able to shine because we did not give up or give in. At some point, we understood that we were doing something for the community, not just for ourselves. These are episodes of our lives that shaped who we are and what we become. The road less traveled produces character, compassion, and an unfaltering belief that there is something greater than what we can see or touch in the world. Out of these experiences came community activists, doctors, lawyers, teachers, and advocates for those who cannot speak for themselves. We clearly came out of this trial with a desire to make the world better, even though the residue lingers. *"If we had known it would be that hard, we might not have done it."*

Today we spend a great deal of time and money researching why our communities, the black communities, are in crisis. We want to figure out where we went wrong and why we have made no progress of any magnitude as a community in over four hundred years of struggle. It is my belief that we must remember where we come from and who brought us if we are going to fix what is broken. The media, the "system" all tell us that black people are generationally bad, dysfunctional, genetically predisposed to lower intellectual achievement than others, especially Caucasians. We have spent a great deal of time swallowing that mess and then wondering why we are dying mentally and physically at a faster rate than anyone else on the planet.

Les Brown says, "Garbage in, garbage stays." The negative we ingest mentally feeds the pariah of bad behavior. When our young people feel that they get more cool points from going to jail than from going to college, it is the parents that need to be checked, not the system. My grandmother, Mary McLeod Bethune, was able to come out of the darkest of places into the light because of who was holding the lantern for her— her parents. The story of my great-grandparents, Samuel and Patsy McLeod, is a story of love and strength that is anchored in the motherland of Africa and cannot be separated from its roots no matter how wide the ocean.

My grandmother held on to that African heritage as she cut new paths for us to follow on, *The Journey*. She stated, "The drums of Africa still beat in my heart." All too often we cut away the roots of the tree and then wonder why it will not bear fruit or maintain life. Like our health-care system, we are more prone to treat the symptom than get to the source of the problem. Historically as a people, we have had to reach our lowest point before we go into action as a unit. We are there now, and I believe that we are beginning to see our path clearer and with a determination to take back what has been stolen. We must save our children if we are to go into the future with any hope of survival.

Scripture tells us that things will get much worse before they get better but that there will be a turning point where good men and women will stand up for what is right and righteous. I believe that *now* is that time. The silence of our collective voices allowed prayer to be taken out of schools, for the educational system to become a warehouse for privatized juvenile centers and prisons with our children being the product to feed that demon. We have long talked about *what* we need to do. Today we need instructive strategies on *how to do* what is necessary to turn the tide.

I am a product of Africa, Gullah Geechee, and Native American Cherokee. My strength is in my DNA as well as how I was indoctrinated along *my Journey*. It prepared me "for such a time as this" so that I shall not fear. It is my duty and responsibility to prepare the "Now" generation as well as future generations for *The Journey* ahead of them. I have endured and overcome obstacles that I never imagined, with courage and strength that I did not know I had until I needed it. I found it within me because of what was poured into me all along the way.

My parents and teachers, both formal and informal, never made me feel that I could not achieve. The minor voices that were naysayers were drowned out by the ones cheering me on. They were overshadowed by the examples that were there for me. *We* must be the examples that our young people need so that they see glimpses of themselves. They must learn to love who they are and be proud of the skin they are in. Black and beautiful, loud and proud, and *prepared* for a world that they must prove themselves in yet today, for the bar is set "twice as good." We can because *they* did and *we must* so that *you* will. Trust God in *all* things and lean not unto your own understanding. Knowledge comes with learning, but wisdom comes with time.

As I looked at my family this past holiday, I was overcome with joy. My sister and brothers, my daughters, my grandson, my nieces and nephews, my grand-nieces and nephews, my cousins—*all* love learning and excel academically and without exception. They are loving and kind. They have willingness to share and a desire to serve community. Even the young ones believe in God and love to praise Him. They understand reverence and what is sacred. Our family is intact, and even when we are out of sync, we love each other deeply. We are overcomers and know the value and urgency of teaching others to do the same. I am grateful every day for the people that God has placed in my circle, and even when I am in a struggle, I still "count it all joy" for God has truly given me strength for *The Journey*.

## Mr. Harold Parker

"For by grace are ye saved through faith; and
that not of yourselves: *it is* the gift of God:
Not of works, lest any man should boast"
(Ephesians 2: 8–9, King James Version).

# I Am Who I Am Because . . .

*Mr. Harold J. Parker, MBA*

# Humble Beginnings

*M*y mother was divorced and left with three children when I was four years old, and we had to stay with my grandparents until they moved to Alamogordo, New Mexico, because my grandfather became the new pastor of the local Baptist Church. Although my father was in the U.S. Army, he never provided my mother with any financial support. I cannot remember him buying birthday or Christmas gifts, let alone providing any financial support. My grandfather was the pastor of Galilee Baptist Church in Roswell, New Mexico, until he became the pastor of a larger church in Alamogordo, New Mexico. Although my grandfather was a pastor, he also owned property and hog farms. He was a lodge member and was an independent carpet installer.

When I started elementary school, my mother always found the time to help me with my homework; and when it came to mathematics, she would always tell me this is how it was taught to me. Two years later, my mother married a military man stationed at Walker AFB, and he is the man I consider to be my dad. My parents instilled honesty, integrity, and a strong work ethic in my psyche.

My father made sure I understood that nothing in life is free and that you can accomplish anything in life if you set goals and work toward their accomplishment. I can remember my dad working during the day and performing numerous part-time jobs (dishwasher and janitor) in the evenings to make ends meet. I actually went with him to the law offices he cleaned at night. I taught the value of money early in life from both my parents and grandparents. My two uncles played a strong role in my early development. Uncle Son (A. T. McCargo Jr.) was a gifted mechanic, great carpenter who built his own house from the ground up when he married a local

Roswell woman. His family moved to Seattle, Washington, shortly after his house was built to work for Volkswagen. He eventually started his own business after he left Volkswagen.

Uncle Carl was the younger of my two uncles, and he had a hot rod and spent a few years on submarines in the U.S. Navy. He would come home and take me to boxing smokers at the navy base. I learned an appreciation for seatbelts before they were in cars when Uncle Carl had to brake, and I hit the windshield and cracked it. I assume I was not injured because I have no memory of going to the doctor. Uncle Carl was also the State Golden Gloves champion for a few years. He eventually left the navy and became a clinical psychologist residing in Springfield, Massachusetts. My aunts would babysit and discipline me when warranted and spoil me as well.

My relatives spent time talking with me and inspiring me. They taught me how to listen and think for myself. My father retired from the United States Air Force (AF), earned his MBA, sold real estate for a few years, and was a professor at Southwest Texas State University. He retired from Texas state government as the regional director for long-term and ambulatory care after my mother passed away. He would always tell me that I would be a great man if I was half the man he was. My parents loved their children and grandchildren and would do anything for them.

My father taught me how to reason through things and determine if I wanted to be a follower or leader depending on the circumstances. My dad would always take the time to explain situations and why things happened to people. He reinforced critical thinking and education as necessary to being instrumental aspects of manhood.

My grandparents loved to keep me with them until I started school. Once school started, they would keep me most weekends, school breaks, and during the summer until my dad was reassigned to Beale AFB, California. I learned from them by asking questions about situations I observed. My grandparents' perspective about life, racial injustice, and politics was sobering and enlightening, considering societal beliefs and stigmas in the 1960s.

## Environmental Influences Associated With My Upbringing

I was truly blessed to begin and end my public education in an integrated school. My family always lived in an integrated neighborhood and it provided me with a different perspective about people, their biases, respective culture and stereotypes.

I began elementary school in Roswell, New Mexico and was never subjected to racial prejudice at the school or my neighborhood. My African American classmates did not reside in my neighborhood but lived in a community adjacent to the railroad tracks. The demographics of my school were predominately Caucasians with a few African Americans and fewer still Mexican Americans. My mother married an Air Force military man while I was in third grade and within a year, we were off to his next assignment at Beale Air Force Base, California.

We lived in Yuba City, California in an integrated neighborhood and I was able to walk to school. My siblings and I were never subjected to racial strife in the neighborhood or at school. There were three African American families; one Asian family, one Mexican American family and the rest were Caucasian families on our block. The children in the neighborhood all played together and were welcome in each other's homes. I would even take my lunch to a Caucasian classmate's home on the lunch break and I was always welcome. However, when I was in fifth grade, I remember a gas station that had a walnut tree, so I stopped to gather the walnuts off the sidewalk and was accused of stealing by the gas station attendant. That was an absurd assertion on his part because I was not on their property. As I reflect back on that incident, I realize that the gas station attendant probably did not like children. That was the only adverse incident I experienced during my elementary school years. Although I was always in an integrated school, I never had any African American teachers until I was in sixth grade. At that time, my home room and music teachers were African American women.

Although I am over 6'2" today, I was short in stature and was less than 6' when I entered the military. I was the eldest of three children and the only male child. My middle school years were sometimes difficult because I was undersized compared to my school mates. When I was in sixth grade, there was an incident where a much larger African American male had me pinned in a corner during lunchtime and a Caucasian neighborhood friend almost hurt him. I had no more trouble with him after that. My neighborhood friend (namesake) asked if I was all right and he went on about his business. My school years in California were uneventful and my father was reassigned to Torrejon Air Base, Spain halfway through my sixth grade year, in 1969.

My middle school years were uneventful until I joined the band in eighth grade and began learning the alto saxophone. I eventually moved up to the tenor saxophone and became first chair through High School. I played in the concert band, jazz band, orchestra, and marching band while in high school.

Racial unrest was never an issue at Torrejon High School (THS) until a handful of African American students from the Deep South arrived during the summer of 1972. They fomented a riot and began assaulting Caucasian students in the hallways in the 1972/1973 school-year. These students from the Deep South had many anger issues from their public school experiences. These students were returned stateside before the 1973 school year was over. Once they were gone, all of the racial unrest at THS stopped. I enjoyed my years at THS and the upper classmen would address many issues during school assemblies. They would enter in dialogues about the *Pledge of Allegiance* and would ask why it should be recited if it was untrue. Guess what, the major proponents asking these questions where Caucasian students. The THS student body agreed to continue reciting the *Pledge of Allegiance* because we believed that one-day the words would be true in America. At the end of my sophomore year after five years in Spain, my father was reassigned to Chanute Air Force Base, Illinois in June, 1973.

The one and one-half years at Rantoul Township High School (RTWPHS) were very enjoyable because I made some good friends and had a couple of friends from THS there also. I enjoyed the band program tremendously, learned to roller skate, drive, found union employment, and a great church. The church had an awesome youth program so I was always occupied. My grandmother became ill in the fall of my senior year and my father was reassigned to San Antonio, Texas. I did my research and asked my dad if I could stay and start the University of Illinois in the summer of 1975. The answer was no. I graduated in May, 1975 from Oliver Wendell Holmes High School in May 1975 and entered the Air Force (AF) in August, 1975. I will be attending 40th year reunions this year for RTWPHS and Oliver Wendell Holmes High School.

My parents always stressed proper English and education. My experience being raised in an integrated environment was a good experience and taught me numerous lessons. I learned that you receive what you put in when it applies to education.

Sure, there were times when being African American counted against me, but overall, a positive outlook and being true to the values I was taught while growing up stood me in good stead. Attitude is like trouble. If you go looking for trouble, it will find you. I also learned that it is easy to be a follower and difficult to be a thinker.

I believe that if you always think about the ramifications of your actions before you act, then you will make the best decision possible, and not be in a reaction mode. I leave you with this: People are judgmental and their first impression is usually a lasting impression, because most times you only have one chance to impress. Initial impressions are difficult to change when they are bad.

My upbringing provided me with a totally different perspective during socially volatile situations. Most times, when culturally diverse people can listen to each other's grievances, the communication process is beneficial to all parties. People should know and understand that it is all right to "agree to disagree," allowing the communication process to continue and not digress.

## Teen-Year Developmental Influences

Interactions between and with both sides of my family taught me the correct method for conflict resolution, proper English usage and diction, self-reliance, positive thinking, reasoning, and how to be a man. I learned many things about history, politics, religion, truth, race relations, and dating by talking to the elders in the family.

I used to cut lawns, shine shoes, babysit, and even cleaned a neighbor's apartment to earn extra money before my sixteenth birthday. Once I turned sixteen, my first job was as a bagger and cashier at Eisner Food Store in Rantoul, Illinois. I had to be a union member in 1973 to work in a grocery store, and I had great benefits. My union experience taught me that sometimes it is not about the salary; it was about the benefits first then the salary.

I learned how to play the alto saxophone in sixth grade and eventually moved to the tenor saxophone. I eventually became first chair and played in the concert, marching, orchestra, and dance bands in middle school and high school. I also joined a local band while residing in Alcala de Henares, Spain, and played my tenor saxophone. I was having a great time, and my mother thought I was growing up too fast since I was fifteen, and the other members of the band were around twenty-one, so I had to leave the group after six to eight months.

I spent my teenage years learning the difference between friends and acquaintances at work and in social settings. Once learned, I was able to recognize individuals for what they were. A friend will always be open and honest with you and never agree with wrongdoing because you are friends.

## Young Adult Value System Influences

With both sides of my family being either Catholic or Baptist and replete with ministers, I learned at an early age to differentiate between church doctrine and what the Bible actually says. This means that just because someone says something, it does not make it true. You only have to watch the news to ascertain this truth. I learned to do my own research and make up my own mind.

Conflict resolution was an important skill learned from my family, friends, church meetings, and colleagues. The most important thing I learned was that it is all right to have a dissenting opinion; however, you must always have a proposed solution. My parents had always explained responsibility and accountability, so I was well prepared when I transitioned into my military career in the AF.

The values I learned at a young age carried over into my AF and consulting career. Throughout my career, I was able to differentiate between leaders and followers and how to select and develop team members. I learned many truths about how to carry myself, to agree to disagree, and to always do your best, regardless of circumstances. During my career, I was an analyst on the space shuttle program, a member of Panama Canal Treaty Implementation Plan handling support agreement issues and concerns for the Department of Defense (DoD); helped draft the Intermediate Nuclear Forces Treaty for Ground-Launched Cruise Missiles with the Soviet Union; a requested panel member for the DoD Worldwide Annual Support Agreement Conference; the Air Combat Command Independent Review officer for Commercial Activities (A-76); helped draft guidance on support agreements, performed economic analyses for Military Construction and Energy Conservation Programs, Military Family Housing, Military Housing Privatization Initiatives, Special Studies and Lifecycle Cost Estimates for numerous acquisition programs; a senior system analyst for antiterrorism and force protection; and performed special cost and financial analysis for other programs. I was also a source selection team member/advisor for myriad acquisition programs while in the AF and later as a consultant.

I enjoyed my time as a military dependent, a member of the AF, and as a consultant. My life and employment experiences taught me the value of integrity, honesty, true friendship, and being true to oneself. It is always a great feeling to be able to view your reflection in the mirror and have no real regrets about your actions or decisions. Always remember that the strength of a person's character is self-evident by their actions and the perception of others.

# How to Prepare the Next Generation

My formative years were spent in the presence of family, friends, colleagues, educators, and church members. Learning honesty, integrity, compassion, and truthfulness were constantly being taught and reinforced my entire life. I am not saying that being truthful or honest was always easy, but it was always the best decision. This way, others always know who you are and what you stand for.

I had to learn from my mistakes and through the mistakes of others. Sometimes those mistakes had penalties, which had to be paid.

Learning about money management and teaching my children how it works is an important part of teaching them responsibility and accountability. Teaching them to make financial decisions was fun and challenging. Ensuring they understood to pay their bills on time or early was always better than being late. Requiring them to read the fine print on credit applications and other accounts would prepare them for the good and bad consequences associated with being timely or tardy.

When your children accept responsibility for their actions and accept the inherent responsibility associated with their decisions, it forces them to realize that an excuse is not acceptable when they are in control of the entire process and making the decision.

I taught them the proper way to make decisions, see all sides of an issue, and assess the impact of their decision on all affected parties. Once they learn decision-making, they begin to understand how to explain their decision without being defensive or insensitive. They also learn that the only credible excuse is one where the failure occurred in a part of the process, which they had no control over.

## Assure the Next Generations Success

Learning to listen to family, friends, colleagues, and educators is the foundation of communicating effectively. It is of paramount importance that you listen and assimilate before you speak. This is an innate character in children that we as individuals should practice.

I am always willing to share my experiences with others while explaining how I learned what I am sharing. I have learned that the wisdom gained from all life experiences is usually replete with trials and tribulations. Some of my wisdom was easy to learn, while some had some hard lessons associated with the gained knowledge.

## Assurance

As individuals, we should always strive to improve things for following generations. We are all victims of circumstance, yet our character is judged by what we do after we suffer a setback. My father taught me that when advice is offered, I must first consider the source, their circumstances, the actual advice, and vet it against my value system before I can judge the true merits of the advice.

Teaching our children to be forthright in their dealings with themselves and others is the ultimate policy. Teaching them that being known as an honest and ethical person is a great accomplishment. I also taught them many people are disingenuous, so it is important that they associate with like-minded individuals and employers.

Harold J. Parker can be contacted via e-mail: pbc_llc_1980@yahoo.com

# References

Ephesians 2: 8–9, King James Version. (n.d.) *The Holy Bible.*

Saint John 3:16, King James Version. (n.d.) *The Holy Bible.*

## Questions (Reflective and Profound)

Based on the racial unrest permeating the media, do you feel that racial discrimination has improved since the 1980s? If yes, how? If no, why not?

_____

_____

_____

_____

_____

Do you feel that the self-oversight on police actions works?

_____

_____

_____

_____

Do you feel that the current checks and balances governing the police, prosecutor, and presiding judges's rulings should be revamped? If so, why?

_____

_____

_____

_____

# *Part 2*

## Believe in Yourself

# Dr. Stan Harris a.k.a. Dr. Breakthrough

II Timothy 2:24–26:

And the servant of the Lord must not strive; but
be gentle unto all men, apt to teach, patient;
In meekness instructing those that oppose
themselves; if God peradventure will give them
repentance to the acknowledging of the truth;
And that they may recover themselves out of the
snare of the devil, who are taken captive by him
at his will.

"Our deepest fear is not that we are inadequate.
Our deepest fear is that we are powerful beyond measure.
It is our light, not our darkness, that most frightens us.
We ask ourselves, who am I to be brilliant, gorgeous,
talented, and fabulous?
Actually, who are you not to be?
You are a child of God.
Your playing small doesn't serve the world.
There's nothing enlightened about shrinking so
that other people won't feel insecure around you.
We are all meant to shine, as children do.
We are born to make manifest the glory of God that is within us.
It's not just in some of us, it's in everyone.
And as we let our own light shine,
we unconsciously give other
people permission to do the same.
As we are liberated from our own fear,
our presence automatically liberates others."
• ~by Marianne Williamson

# "Every Master Was Once a Mess; Therefore, Every Mess Can Become a Master"

*Dr. Stan Harris a.k.a. Dr. Breakthrough*

*T*hrough Mentorship." The very title itself should excite and encourage you because, truthfully, every person that you admire, respect, or look up to, believe it or not, they were not always the way you see them now. It may be hard to conceive it, but your heroes and sheroes were not always the shining examples and stars that they are now. So my whole purpose is to empower you or to equip you to empower others so they will no longer stay in mediocrity but actually live out their full potential or what I like to call, "become the star you really are in God's eyes."

God called Gideon a mighty man of valor (Judges 6:12) while he was hiding from the enemy. God looks at us not as we are but for what we can and will be when we obey Him and follow His path for our lives. Jeremiah was called to be a prophet unto the nations when he was just a child, and he reminded God that he was only a child, but God saw him as a mighty prophet. (Jeremiah 1: 5–8, KJV). Many people (stars) shrink back and even refuse to let their light shine because they assume they need to become perfect before they can be used of God or do much good. As a matter of fact, your imperfections might just make you perfect for the job you are called to do.

One reason people procrastinate is because they are waiting for the perfect time, perfect situation, etc., but it never comes; and if it did, we would miss it because we are not perfect. As a minister of the gospel, I jokingly tell people, "If you ever find a perfect church, don't join in it because you will ruin it." I'm not perfect obviously, but my wife Nadia is close to perfect; however, we tell people, "We are perfect for each other." So my greatest breakthrough on procrastination came when I seemed to hear the Lord saying to my spirit, "You don't necessarily have to get it right. You just have to get it going, and once you get it going, I'll help you get it right!"

Did you know it's almost impossible to steer a car as long as it's sitting still? But once it moves, it's very easy to steer. As a matter of fact, a car sitting still doesn't need to be steered, thus God doesn't or won't direct you until you get moving. Decide now to move instantly despite of your fears or feelings of not knowing everything ahead of time. This reminds me of a quote by Pablo Picasso: "I am always doing that which I cannot do, in order that I may learn how to do it."

The great Dr. Martin Luther King Jr. said, "You don't have to see the whole staircase, just take the first step and keep stepping." So let me state again, "Every mess can be a master through mentorship, pressure, and time." Noah got drunk, Rahab was a harlot, Jacob was a manipulator, and Peter cursed and denied the Lord. Mary got pregnant out of wedlock, Thomas was a doubter, David committed adultery, Paul killed Christians, and Moses even murdered a man. Now what's your problem again? Even when Jesus came, he spent time with the down and outers instead of the religious high and mighty crowd. He called his disciples from among the outcast of society. Matthew, the tax collector, hated by most; Peter, the loud, foul mouthed fisherman; Mary Magdalene, the impure woman . . . Must I go on?

Once (and sometimes while) your transformation takes place, your mess becomes part of the message needed most by the masses. Remember, every master was at once a mess! We all start out as babies in life messing on ourselves, and someone else has to clean us and teach us. Great speakers were not born speaking great; they were either once shy or scared to speak, but they broke through their fears and insecurities. The best business owners were not always great at business; they had to learn. Again, let me say, "Every master was at once a mess, therefore every mess can become a master especially through mentorship!"

I love II Timothy 2:24–26 because he starts out saying, "And the servant of the Lord must not strive . . ." You see God's servants may be miracle workers in your eyes, but they are just servants! Yes, God calls His apostles, evangelists, pastors, teachers, prophets, etc., servants. This doesn't take away from their lofty positions or dishonor them in any way. It just helps His other servants, perhaps like you who may not hold the titles, etc., but just realize that they are simply servants who are given the task of "instructing those who oppose themselves" (v. 25a). Wow, what a powerful statement and awesome task to instruct those who oppose themselves!

I dare say most of us oppose ourselves without realizing what we are doing. We think we are being humble, but in essence, whenever you do not let your light shine by living out your highest potential, you are missing out on God's best. In II Timothy 2:25b, it says, "If God peradventure will give them repentance to the acknowledging of the truth." So this means God will help you change your mind, and when your mind has been changed, you can now acknowledge the truth, which is, you are a special person made by God to shine, thus the book title *Shining Stars!*

So many people try to hide or shrink back because they fail to realize that they are and have a gift from God, thus He wants them to shine. Today I travel all over the world preaching the Gospel while also performing martial arts demonstrations, etc. I have spoken in all fifty states and twenty-seven countries speaking to crowds as large as seventeen thousand people, but you should have seen me when I started! I was a mess when I started, scared to death, so unsure of myself; I only started because others saw something in me, believed in me, and encouraged me. I want to do that now for others and help them know that they can breakthrough their shell and become shining stars that give light to others and point to the glory of God.

You must realize that my life was such a mess, but God uses us not because of us but rather in spite of us!

My dad left when I was only three years of age, and he never called or sent Mom any money. When I was just six years of age, I was out in the field playing by myself until I noticed a gang of teenagers coming my way. I was scared; one of them punched me in the stomach, while another hit me in the face. They threw me on the ground, and all of them started stomping me like I was an ant or roach. I was bleeding from everywhere you could bleed, but still they weren't done. One of the teens took a bucket of tar and poured it on my face, while others threw feathers on me! There I lay, a little boy beaten, bruised, bloody, tarred and feathered. Thank God someone found me and rushed me to the hospital.

I lived through verbal, racial, physical, and sexual abuse! I tried to commit suicide on two occasions, and I'm so glad I failed. Someone said, "Suicide is a permanent solution to a temporary problem." I never dreamed that I could become and do the things I do today, so that's why I love speaking and writing to empower people that you can breakthrough their low self-esteem, poverty, procrastination, fear, and doubt to become a mighty star for God who shines bright!

Mentorship, by the way, is the fastest and easiest way to reach your potential and increase your shine power revealing the star you really are!

Socrates mentored Plato.
Plato mentored Aristotle.
Aristotle mentored Alexander the Great.

Andrew Carnegie mentored Napoleon Hill.
Napoleon Hill mentored W. Clement Stone.
W. Clement Stone mentored Jack Canfield.
Benjamin Graham mentored Warren Buffett.

William E. Bailey mentored Les Brown
Les Brown mentored thousands.
Bill Bailey also mentored Jim Rohn.
Jim Rohn mentored Tony Robbins.
Tony Robbins mentored millions.

Moses mentored Joshua.
Joshua mentored the Israelites.
Elijah mentored Elisha.
Elisha mentored at the school of the prophets.
Elisha also mentored the widow woman.

Paul mentored young Timothy.
Timothy mentored the Church of Ephesus.
Jesus mentored the Disciples.

Now the best part, Jesus told them, "The works that I do shall ye do also, and greater works than these shall ye do . . ." (John 14:12 KJV). So the person being mentored cannot just do what the mentor did but actually exceed or double what the mentor accomplished! I often say, "If you believe like I believe and do like I do, then what happens for me can happen for you, but because I'm not the standard, it can happen even better for you." And by the way, that's my desire and prayer that those whom I mentor will far exceed what I have done!

Once when I was speaking in Florida and Joshua, my oldest son, was with me, some people thought that they were being complimentary of me by telling Joshua, "If you could just become half the man, your dad is you will be a wonderful young man." I pulled Joshua aside and said, "Son, those people meant well, but they were so wrong. My goal is not for you to be half the man I am but perhaps twice the man I am because I will teach you all I know, plus God will give you even more." I said, "Joshua, I would like nothing more than for you and your brothers and sister to double my accomplishments because your mom and I have laid the foundation, so you all can build a wonderful super structure." This is why Jeremiah 5:5 (KJV) says, "I will get me to the great men who have known the way of the Lord."

Solomon teaches us in Proverbs 27:17: "Iron sharpeneth iron; so a man sharpeneth the countenance of his friend." I love Proverbs 13:20 (KJV): "He that walketh with wise men shall be wise, but a companion of fools shall be destroyed."

So may I ask you a question? Why are you or why do people spend so much time with people who make fun of them for doing right or who belittle them for wanting to reach their dreams, goals, or aspirations? Surround yourself with empowering people, books, etc., so you can become the star you really are. Did you know that stars give light and direction? Thus your life can be a great source of hope and help to others. I was blessed to marry the woman of my dreams, Nadia MeChelle Harris, whom I call my ABCD, which stands for Adorable, Brown, Caramel, Delight", and we say we "aspire to inspire breakthroughs even after we have expired!"

**My question to the reader:** So what will you change as a result of reading this chapter? Are you willing to commit to letting your light shine brighter for good and for God?

Extra thought-provoking question: "If *you* died today, do know for sure that you would go to Heaven, or would you have some doubt?

Let me quickly share with you what someone shared with me many years ago because actually, the only light we have is the Lord himself! Psalm 27: 1 says, "The LORD *is* my *light* and my salvation . . ." It's like the little girl in Sunday school years ago while listening to the teacher talk about the bigness and strength of God. The little girl raised her hand and asked a simple but profound question: "Since God is as strong and as big as you say He is, and if He is in our little hearts, shouldn't He be sticking out all over the place?" Wow, that is the essence of this chapter and the entire book, but he can't stick out unless you have allowed him to come in. Revelation 3:20 says, "Behold I stand at the door and knock, if any man opens the door, I will come in . . ." So perhaps you can't shine the reflection of God if you have never invited Him into your heart.

February 14, 1976, as a fifteen-year-old boy, people knocked on my door and showed me what we call the Romans Road to Salvation. First, in essence, they showed me that I was a sinner. Romans 3:10 says, "As it is written, there is none righteous, no, not one." And Romans 3:23 says, "For all have sinned and come short of the glory of God." Second, they showed me that being a sinner I would have to pay for my sins by going to the lake of fire and become separated from God forever! Romans 6:23a says, "For the wages of sin is death . . ." Revelation 21:8 says, "But the fearful, and unbelieving, and the abominable, and murderers, and whoremongers, and sorcerers, and idolaters, and all liars shall have their part in the lake which burneth with fire and brimstone: which is the second death. Third, they helped me realize that every sinner has to pay the penalty of their sin, but Jesus came to save us. According to Romans 5:8, "But God commandeth his love toward us, in that, while we were yet sinners, Christ died for us." Fourth, they taught me that if I would repent and believe that Jesus died, was buried, and arose again to take my place, He would give me His gift of eternal life! Romans 6:23b says, "But the gift of God is Eternal Life through Jesus Christ our Lord." They showed me Romans 10:9–10:

"That if thou shalt confess with thy mouth the Lord Jesus, and shalt believe in thine heart that God hath raised him from the dead, thou shalt be saved. For with the heart man believeth unto righteousness; and with the mouth confession is made unto salvation."

Then they showed me Romans 10:13: "For whosoever shall call upon the name of the Lord shall be saved." They then asked me *if I* wanted to be saved, and of course, I said yes! I got on my knees and prayed a simple prayer of faith: "Father, I know I have sinned. Please forgive me. I believe that Jesus died and rose again, and I ask you to save me and give me your gift of eternal life in Jesus name. Amen."

Praise God that day I got saved; I got born again. I received the gift of eternal life and the light of God was rekindled in my heart. So what about you? Right now, ask Him to come into your heart, ask Him to save you and give you His gift of eternal life. When you do it, the light of God begins to shine through you! Do it now and let me know about it. Dr. Stan Harris 717-275-3508 or e-mail DrBreakTo@gmail.com. I John 5:13: "These things have I written unto you that believe on the name of the Son of God; that ye may know that ye have eternal life, and that ye may believe on the name of the Son of God. Once you ask Him to save you, by faith you can now know that you have eternal life and that Heaven will one day be your home and now the light of God can shine through you!"

Philippians 2:15 (KJV): "That ye may be blameless and harmless, the sons of God, without rebuke, in the midst of a crooked and perverse nation, *among whom ye shine as lights in the world.*"

*Mrs. Paula R. Bryant*

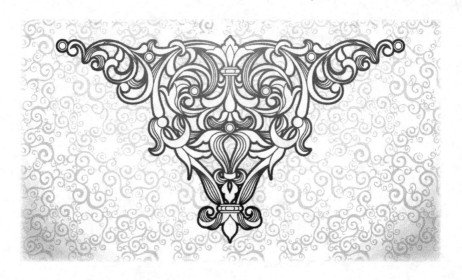

My God will meet all your needs according
To his glorious riches in Christ Jesus.
Philippians 4:19

# Becoming Who You Are

*Mrs. Paula R. Bryant*

*R*ecently, a dynamic friend of mine had a get together for "the girls" at her home, at which a surprise was waiting for everyone who walked in the door. Each guest was greeted by a mirror and a message that said, "If this isn't you, don't come in." I rolled with laughter when she told me about it because I wasn't able to attend and experience her front-door surprise firsthand. But my friend had a purpose. She wanted everyone to come in, put everything aside, and just be themselves. *But why should we have to be reminded to be who we really are?* It should be natural, effortless for us to walk through the lifelong process of becoming who we have been created to be—so what gets in the way? Life happens. People hurt us. We experience failure. We become distracted and disconnected from others and from the source of our life and purpose. When the challenges of life get us off track, we stop becoming who we are destined to be.

Don't get me wrong. It is understandable to pause from time to time when we experience challenges and/or setbacks. But stopping isn't an option. Stopping means that we become more focused on the problem than on the solution. It means that we shut down and get stuck in a place where we've been hurt, offended, or have fallen short, instead of coming to terms with the issue and moving beyond it.

Now let me be clear. Regardless of what we have achieved in our lives up to this point, we are each still in the process of becoming. So whether you are male or female, married or single, young or old, if you are living and breathing, there is still more of you to be revealed. You are still becoming. You could be a student or a teacher, a CEO or an employee of a corporation, retired or at the pinnacle of your career . . . You haven't tapped into everything you are capable of. This is the way God saw fit to design the human experience. Every day you open your eyes, you still have more to become and accomplish.

The word *become* is a verb. It means "to come, change, or grow to be."[1] [[REF]] In a positive sense, *becoming who we are*—who we have been created to be—implies that we are constantly taking action, developing, and moving forward to reach our fullest potential. But if we're stuck in one place, moving backward, or are constantly repeating the same negative patterns, we're becoming less than what we're intended to be. I'm writing this chapter not because I'm "all that and a bag of chips" but because I have learned valuable lessons from being stuck in places the Lord ultimately had to lead me out of. Why? Because I didn't always see everything clearly, and when I did, too often I wasn't bold enough to step out, confront issues, and overcome them.

I have faced my share of challenges on my journey as a believer, wife, mother, grandmother, writer/editor, minister, and entrepreneur. There have even been times when years, after the fact, I had to go back and revisit areas of my life where I had subconsciously pressed the "stop button." Do you relate? No one is exempted from stopping, not me, and not even you—because not one of us has fully arrived. Often we are accomplished in some areas, while other areas of our lives are stopped at a crossroad. *As you read this chapter, consider where you are in your process of becoming. Which areas of your life do you need to revisit so that you can release that "stop button" by taking action, developing, and moving forward?*

## Moving Beyond What Other People See

My deepest challenges to understanding and becoming who I am started early in my life. I was in elementary school in Denver, Colorado, when I had my first experience outside of home that really confused me about how other people saw me. I'll never forget it. A couple of girls came up to me one day and said another girl wanted to fight me because I had called her a "nigger." I was shocked. Not only was I not the kind of person who had fights or who even talked like that, but something also troubled me even more. *But I'm black,* I remember saying to myself. *Why would she think that I called her that name?* Obviously, my accuser didn't see me that way, and neither did the girls who had brought me her message.

I can still remember what she looked like. She had beautiful deep brown skin and long, thick hair that ran past her shoulders, which she usually wore braided in pony tails. On the other hand, my skin looked like pale butterscotch, and my hair was long, fine, and bouncy curly. But up until that day, I had never seen myself as being anything other than black. And it wasn't until that day that I realized many people of my own race thought I wasn't black at all.

As I went through school in Colorado, I became used to being called high yellow or white girl by some black people, while some whites and kids of other races saw me as being black. But it seemed no matter who I was with—black, white, or otherwise—they usually didn't see me as being one of them, at least not as it concerned my race. Then in my early twenties, I moved to New York City and discovered a much bigger world. Interestingly, the majority of people I met didn't think I was black or white; they thought I was Puerto Rican, French, or some other ethnicity. But I got tired of being labeled depending on how different people saw me. By that time, I knew that along with being black, I had Indian and white blood in my heritage. So though my U.S. birth certificate didn't state my race—I'm a naturalized citizen—I settled within myself (and told anyone who asked me) that I was a "bli-nite." That caught people off guard, and it got a lot of laughs; but interestingly, many people related better to the mixed race I came up with instead of thinking of me as being black.

When I applied for college in New York, I mischievously checked "Other" as my race on the application, only it backfired on me. A couple of months later, after registering for my classes the following semester, I discovered that someone at the school had taken the liberty to change my race on my school records. Unbeknownst to me, years after that first incident in elementary school, somebody else had decided that I was white, only this time it was on record and "official." Once again, I was shocked at what people saw when they looked at me on the surface. But when I looked in the mirror, I honestly didn't see that I could possibly be white— but apparently, other people did.

Looking at my African American heritage, there are a lot of historic "firsts" in my family. My father was an officer and pilot in the air force, was part of one of the first black groups at Tuskegee Air Base involved in learning to fly, was part of the first black air force pursuit squadron in World War II, retired a lieutenant colonel after twenty-five years of service, and then became a Civil Rights investigator for the state of Colorado. My mother's father, James H. Morton, Sr., was a chemistry professor at Sam Huston College, was elected president of the Austin NAACP branch in 1946. In that capacity, he attended a meeting of student organizations at the University of Texas in Austin that (as reported by a major Dallas newspaper) was the first time students came together and publically supported admitting black students to UTA. He later became the NAACP's state lobbyist. In 1977, my aunt Azie, who married my mother's brother, Jimmy Morton, Jr., became the first black woman to be appointed as treasurer of the United States by Pres. Jimmy Carter.

There is a rich history in my family, but I wasn't aware of a number of these things until much later in my life. So from the time the incident occurred in elementary school, I always felt different from my friends, and then I went through a season of throwing my hands up in the air and declaring to everyone who didn't see me as being black that I was who *I said* I was. Now I'm at peace with being a light-skinned African American woman who also has Indian and some degree of European blood in my heritage. I also understand, although this issue affected me, it didn't start with me. It goes back two hundred-plus years to when blacks were separated (inside versus outside) on plantations. Since then, many generations have passed, and a number of African Americans have other bloodlines that are part of their heritage. But looking on the surface, it's just more obvious in my case.

*What about you? Do you now or have you ever felt labeled by the way other people see you on the surface? If so, does this distract you as you go about your daily life? Does it affect how you relate, respond, or react to others?* If your answer to any of these questions is *yes*, then you have more to discover in your process of becoming. You are who you are and look the way you look for a purpose. This purpose is higher, and it goes much deeper than the texture of your hair or the color of your skin.

## Moving Beyond What You Can See

I might not have been as confused and troubled about my ethnicity growing up if I wasn't facing even greater challenges at home. A far more debilitating issue started before I went to elementary school when my mother had what I remember being told was a "nervous breakdown." This term is no longer used like it was during the 1960s, but it describes what happens when a person becomes overwhelmed by the demands of life and, for a period, can't function normally. Unfortunately, this one-time occurrence turned into a lifelong mental disorder for my mother that worsened with time.

I was four or five years old when the first of many episodes I would never forget took place. My father, brother, two sisters, and I went to see my mother at a mental facility where she was staying for in-patient treatment. Shortly after we arrived, she walked into the big "living room" area where we were waiting; but when she saw me, she didn't know who I was. That was extremely traumatic for me. I couldn't reconcile it in my young mind. I wasn't thinking that my mother was probably on some type of medication or had had a treatment that affected her memory. I just wondered why my mommy didn't know me; why she didn't want to hold me or kiss me. And being the youngest child, I didn't talk to anyone about what I was feeling. I held it inside.

My mother ultimately returned home with her memory restored, but her emotional condition didn't improve. Then later, in what I can only imagine were last resort decisions, my mother had two separate psychosurgeries called partial lobotomies. In this controversial procedure, most of the connections to and from the frontal lobe of the brain are cut or scraped away. This blunts the emotions, usually tension and anxiety, in an attempt to change or control the patient's behavior. But sadly, there can be serious long-term side effects. My mother was somewhat more functional emotionally after those surgeries, but she was never the same.

As a result, for most of my life, living with my mother was like walking a tightrope or trying to walk on eggshells. She went from being nervous all the time to becoming aggressive. The slightest action taken or the smallest word spoken at the wrong moment set her off emotionally. When she was upset, there was no comforting her. In fact, whoever was closest to her when something set her off would become the target of her anger and frustration. We all had different ways of coping with the constant verbal and sometimes physical attacks. For me, retreating into myself and suppressing my feelings and many things I wanted to say or do became normal. I did almost anything to keep the peace and avoid experiencing another blowup, including taking the blame for things I didn't do. I didn't realize this was forming a pattern of thinking and behavior in me that I would have to confront and overcome later in my life.

Adding to our family's dilemma, my father was burdened with raising four children and providing for the family on his own. A highly disciplined man, he worked hard, cooked, cleaned, and expected my brother and sisters and me to do the same. We knew he loved us, but he wasn't nurturing; he was firm, disciplined, and perfectionistic. As a child growing up, I didn't understand what he was going through or why he couldn't give me what I needed emotionally. So although I knew my father was there for me and that my mother was sick and not able to love me the way she otherwise would have, I was developing an empty space in my soul. Even though I was well taken care of, I didn't feel accepted or affirmed by either of my parents. This became another issue that suppressed my potential, one that I would ultimately have to face and deal with.

After years of negative conditioning, I pressed multiple "stop buttons" in my life and became a person who first and foremost wanted to please others. I was afraid to say what I really thought or do what I really wanted to do because I was worried about what other people would think of me. When I was curious, I avoided asking questions. When a problem came up, I immediately felt guilty, even if I didn't create the problem. I was self-conscious and often froze up around people, especially authority figures: bosses, pastors, and so on, when there was no reason for me to feel that way. I willingly gave up being properly acknowledged for things I had worked hard developing because that felt more natural than conducting myself in a way that assured my contributions were recognized. At times in my life, I even did things that were against my own values because I had formed a habit of seeking acceptance and approval and avoiding confrontation. All in all, for many years I settled for less when I could have achieved and realized more. But that wasn't who I really was. The person I had been created to become was smothered underneath layers of hurts, failures, and insecurities.

In order to become who I was created to be, I had to come through a process of revisiting and moving beyond what I could see in each area. In some cases, this took years. The same is true for you, whether your situation was or is like mine, or if it's completely different. So let me ask you: *did any issues come to the surface in your mind as you read through this section? If so, have you faced and dealt with each one, or are some of them resolved while others still linger beneath the surface in your mind?* Often our lives show us what we haven't dealt with because as I said before, at the same time we're accomplished in one area we're stopped at a crossroad in another.

## Moving into How God Sees You

I accepted the Lord when I was a teenager, but immaturity and a lot of emotional baggage kept me from giving myself to Him completely. However, in the midst of my mess early in my twenties, the Lord reached out to me through a friend I worked with. For some reason that I couldn't begin to understand, she refused to give up on me. She was a believer, and no matter what crazy story I told her about things I'd done, she never stopped being my friend. A year or so after we became friends, she invited me to an event at Brooklyn Tabernacle where a man named David Wilkerson was speaking. That night the Lord made Himself real to me. As the music and singing began, the Holy Spirit touched my heart. He exposed a "stop button" in my soul, and tears started flowing from my eyes. There was nothing I could do to stop them. I knew God was causing this to happen because, growing up, church was the place where we had to look our "Sunday best" and be on our best behavior. Crying or doing anything distracting wasn't an option. But that night I couldn't restrain myself. And by the end of the evening, I rededicated my life to God.

The first area the Lord immediately led me to change was my relationship with my boyfriend. But at that point in time, although I thought I had sincerely given my life to the Lord, I hadn't yet given Him my whole heart. I also didn't understand that when God prompted me to do something, He would give me the ability to do it . . . if I chose to obey Him. Long story short, I started attending the church and took a stand with my boyfriend about having sex before marriage. He even ended up coming to church with me—but I didn't keep my stand. When he put pressure on me, I folded. I loved him and was afraid that I would lose him. You see, at that time, I struggled seeing myself the way God saw me. I only saw the person I was before God made Himself real to me. As a result, my boyfriend was my first priority. He had my whole heart, and God came in second.

We can't be in a close relationship with God and become everything He has created us to be if our heart is divided, if other people or things are more important to us than He is. God wants us to give ourselves to Him completely—body, soul, and spirit—because His process of *becoming who we are* encompasses our entire being. It makes an impact in every aspect of our lives all the days of our lives.

Ultimately, I gave myself to the Lord completely. By that point, my boyfriend and I had moved to Texas and were thinking about getting married. God made Himself real to me again, this time, while I was getting my sister's car detailed (of all places). He did it through a girl who was shining my shoes (which was a first for me). As she started talking, she casually started telling me about how good Jesus was. I listened intently, even agreed, but I was confused about how the Holy Spirit was supposed to work in my life. This had hindered my walk with God. Well, every time a question came up in my mind, she immediately answered it—and I never said a word! I couldn't deny that God had designed that moment. I couldn't deny that even though I had failed Him time and time again, He was reaching out to me and telling me exactly what I needed to know to get back on track.

That Sunday, September 9, 1984, I went to church with my new friend and gave my heart to the Lord . . . completely. Before I walked up to the altar, I decided that I wanted God, even if it meant I would lose my boyfriend. That released the "stop button" I had pressed in New York after rededicating my life to the Lord. As God would have it, my boyfriend took me back to be baptized that evening, and that's when I broke the news that we could no longer be intimate unless we were married. He resisted at first, no doubt thinking back to what had happened in New York, but this time I obeyed God, and He helped me to keep my stand. Within two weeks, my boyfriend moved out. Then about a month later, in his car on the side of a highway, he genuinely gave his heart to the Lord. Suddenly, although I had been avoiding him, my ex-boyfriend and I started running into each other in the least likely places. My head was spinning. We started talking again and then dating—God's way. When we asked the Lord to confirm if He wanted us to get married, He confirmed it over and over again.

It's amazing to think of everything God has done in our lives since we both gave ourselves fully to the Lord. Things I never imagined I'd even think about or do. But it would take a book, not just a chapter, to tell you about it all. Now after thirty years of marriage, two children, and seven grandchildren, my husband Kim is still my boyfriend, and he's so much more!

## Who You Are Begins with God

There's something to be said about God's primary role in helping us to become who we are. There's something to be said about learning how to not put the cart before the horse. In other words, we have to learn how to keep our priorities straight—seeking an intimate relationship with God first—so that He can change our hearts, transform our minds, and make us the best we can be. Here's a promise from the Bible: "And all of us, as with unveiled face, [because we] continued to behold [in the Word of God] as in a mirror the glory of the Lord, are constantly being transfigured into His very own image in ever increasing splendor and from one degree of glory to another; [for this comes] from the Lord [Who is] the Spirit" (II Corinthians 3:18, Amplified Bible).[2] [[REF]]

So you see, no one has arrived, but everyone—no matter what they have achieved—is still in the process of becoming. And when we belong to God, this process progressively unfolds as we seek and obey Him toward reaching a much higher potential than any of us could reach on our own.

I have traveled around the world and realized that by God's design, although I have a rich heritage as an African American woman, I could live any number of places and be received as a local. And because I grew up painfully aware of how other people saw me, I don't judge others by what I see on the surface. I look deeper and try to discover their uniqueness. When I encounter people who are going through painful issues, instead of writing them off, my heart goes out to them. And when I encounter someone who is young in his or her walk with God, I now see them through the eyes of understanding.

As I have walked through my process of becoming, the Lord has allowed me to discover and develop gifts and skills He placed within me. He has released the creativity that I suppressed as a child and has used it to help develop and publish books that have made an impact on multiple thousands of lives around the world. As I trust and obey the Lord, He is taking all my pain and turning it into purpose. Can I tell you again that the same is true for you?

Think about how gracious God has been to you in your lifetime, how He has been with you in both good and difficult times, even when you weren't aware of it. The things you have suffered in the past and the challenges you now face don't have to keep you from becoming who you are and reaching your God-given potential—because He is in the process of transforming your pain into purpose. Romans 8:28 puts it this way, "We are assured and know that [God being a partner in their labor] all things work together and are [fitting into a plan] for good to and for those who love God and are called according to [His] design and purpose" (Amplified Bible).[3] [[REF]]

Now let's think again about what it means to become and restate the definition: to *become*, we have to *change* in order to *grow*. Your scars can be turned into shining stars as you trust the Lord, do what He leads you to do, and release the "stop buttons" in your life. As long as you're living and breathing, your fullest potential awaits you!

End Notes

[1] "Become," dictionary.reference.com/browse/become?s=t. Accessed 1/26/15.

[2] The *Amplified Bible*, WORDsearch® Bible 10. Powered by LifeWay. Build 10.6.0.81. All rights reserved.

[3] Ibid.

Mr. Hasaan Rasheed, M.Ed.

Seek first his kingdom and his
Righteousness, and all these things will
Be given to you as well.
Matthew 6:33

# Tell Me That I won't and I'll show you that I Will

*Mr. Hasaan Rasheed, M.A.Ed.*
Arkansas Baptist College Professor/Assistant Track Coach
Philander Smith Adjunct Professor/Assistant Track Coach
Owner-Total Body Fitness Training LLC
President/CEO- All My God Sons, Inc.
Memphis Grizzlies Acrobatic dunk Team

*N*othing great comes easy. The mentality of a highly motivated individual was sparked around the year 1994. I was only 6 years of age when I stumbled upon a movie called "Richie Rich", starring Macaulay Culkin. This movie depicted a young boy who had all the riches that anybody could ever ask for, but soon realized that no amount of money could buy happiness. At this point in life I realized my family was not the most fortunate when it came to finances and having all the material things that my peers seemed to thrive on. What I did know was that both my parents were educated, hard workers, and did what they had to do for my brothers and me to have food and a roof over our head. While most of my friends at that age were out buying shoes, clothes, and shiny jewelry, I chose to save and invest my money towards a better situation. Being the oldest sibling of three in the house hold kept me in the mindset that I would have to work for my own things if I wanted to have it. I also had older siblings from my dad's side that were encouraging and showed me what routes of life I should not travel down to keep myself successful. The inspiration I gained from watching "Richie Rich" broadened my horizons on what I too could be capable of at a young age. Dreaming this big at my age seemed to be uncommon and boring to most of my peers. So I stayed dormant until I saw the right opportunity to present my visions to the world. I knew deep within my leadership and business mentality would take me far beyond my wildest dreams.

*Started studying for the SAT in 5th grade.

Let us fast forward to the year 2001. I was 13 in the 8th grade with my mind set on taking over the world. Little did I know it would also be the year of a summer to spark some of my future success. At this point in life I was dressing apart from my classmates and setting standards for a new dress attire. As my peers would ask, "Who are you trying to impress with your church boy clothes on?" My response was one that they could not quite comprehend yet. I learned in middle school how to turn negative criticism into positive energy that would later influence many. This also happened to be the year of the 9/11 attacks in Washington, D.C. and New York City. This event not only shocked the nation but changed the rest of my days of living as well. Imagine being this young with a name so close to the terrorist leader who changed the nation with his influence. I quickly had to develop a back bone to the ignorance of my peers with their jokes and inability to open their eyes to understanding more then what was seen on television. I quickly began to realize who true friends were and how the people of this nation were so blinded because of their own lack of research and knowledge. It occurred to me that many just feared what they didn't understand and were too lazy to want to understand anything outside what they were accustomed to learning. Growing up with two religious views in my family gave me all the knowledge I needed to be prepared for this moment and to help many understand how to be outside the box. Once everybody noticed that words would not stir me, they decided to join me in learning more. It was funny to start seeing peers try to dress like me and ask for my opinion on what they looked like. This is the year where I developed the mentality to not care about what everybody else had to say about me. I would be an inventor, motivator, dreamer, and leader.

My first mission within this year led me on a path of wanting to start college early and open my own business. So I took up an entrepreneur college class at Paul Quinn College to test the waters on what it would be like taking college level classes at such a young age. I learned quite a bit about business and everything my father had been trying to cram into my brain in earlier years. Growing up watching my dad hustle from job to job and run his own company is where I get my entrepreneur spirit from. He never made it easy for me to get where I was going and always had a lesson behind it when I would reach my destination. There were many times in my earlier life that I would question if any other kid my age had to read books on business and learn about other successful owners. Although it seemed like punishment, I knew that somehow it would be intertwined with the level of success I wanted to be on. So I kept pushing forward and continued to soak in as much knowledge as my brain allowed me to process. Taking on this summer college entrepreneur class was me putting some of these lessons to the test. During this particular summer we also took a family vacation on touring Historically Black Colleges and Universities. My parents instilled in all of my siblings the importance of education at young ages so that we could already have an idea of what we wanted to do with our lives. It was during this particular that I had determined I would later become a Morehouse Man. Learning about the history of the college, the important leaders who went here, and the geographic location, helped me to decide that when my time came this would be the best fit for a future leader such as myself.

Entrepreneurship 101 at Paul Quinn College was a pivotal point in the making of my success. Not only did I learn how to implement everything, but it also led me to turn a vision into a reality. During the summer we had to do a final project on a hypothetical business we would open if given the opportunity rite away. I decided since it was summer and scorching hot, snow cones would be something worth looking in to. We were already on a campus full of summer programs that were consumed with kids from all around the city. As a kid with my business ideas flowing I knew that I would need to produce something that could cater to kids who would beg their parents to have some of what I was selling. This would draw in the kids because of something to cool them off and would also give the parents something to quench their own thirst. After presenting this project to my other colleagues and doing some research, I decided that this project should become a reality. Like anything else business orientated, I would need to seek the counseling of my father who I knew could show me the starter path to actually make this an official company in the business system. My very first company was born that summer, Snow Cone Island Incorporated. I opened in Paul Quinn gymnasium a week after my Entrepreneur class ended. My crowd consisted of kids in summer programs along with parents that picked them up in the late afternoon. It was at that moment in my life I understood the true meaning of making big things happen if you put your mind to it.

* (High School) Started a project on freedom Riders and turned it into a movement at 16 years and hustled fruit snacks to help pay car note and help provide food for the family.

*(College – Present)

Graduated and did whatever it took to get through Morehouse.

Oprah Winfrey Scholar. All American Track. Training Clients in College.. ex. Jasmine Sadet .Hustled side jobs to keep multiple incomes

*Bought first house at 21(junior year of college). Many told me it couldn't happen.

*Journey to Little Rock, Arkansas to see my youngest brother through college and see what I could do to better myself and help to grow this city.

*Youngest College Professor when I got to Little Rock, Arkansas (Check Dates)

*Shot Down from the original job at Philander Smith. And two more positions after that when I first moved.

*Worked as Assistant general manager for a training company for a little over a year. Bad leadership drove me to later open my own Training Company (Total Body Fitness Training LLC.) and Boys Nonprofit (All My God Sons, INC.

## Dr. Shirley Clark

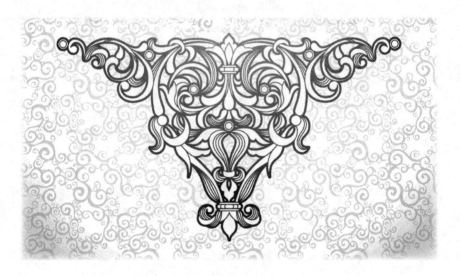

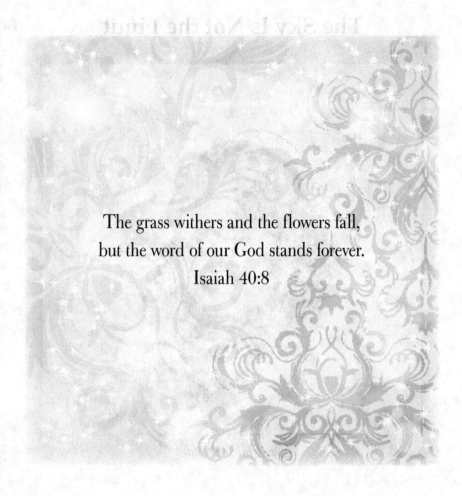

The grass withers and the flowers fall,
but the word of our God stands forever.
Isaiah 40:8

# The Sky Is Not the Limit

*Dr. Shirley Clark*

*I*t was a day I would never forget. It was my high school graduation. As the great Charles Dickens's novel said, "It was the best of times and the worst of times." I was seventeen, and I was quite ignorant to all that was going on around me during this time. I had very little insight about my graduation and education as a whole. All I knew was that it was expected of me to finish high school, but completing it had no real long-term meaning in my life. You see, the entire seventeen years of my life, I was reared in an impoverished environment. My mother had only an eighth-grade education, and I don't really think she knew why I needed to finish high school, no more than it was expected of a child.

When my mother and father married, they were sixteen years old. They lived in a rural community down on the East Coast, Washington, NC. Everybody in the community mostly worked in fields planting and harvesting mostly corn, collard greens, and tobacco. Even now, I can still see myself working in tobacco barns, gathering, and tying tobacco to be placed on a pole. So when my parents married at such a young age, they had to forfeit their education to work to create a life for themselves.

A year later, their lives were challenged more as they begin having children. Every year following for four years, they had a child. After a one-year break, they had four more children. One did not live, but as you can imagine, taking care of all of us was a real challenge. But everything went from bad to worse when my father starting drinking, so I was told.

Being the youngest child in the family, I don't remember these years much, but my older siblings did. They have shared with me that when my daddy would drink, occasionally, he would become so enraged that he would physically abuse my mother. This went on for years, until my mother made the decision to leave my daddy.

I was five years old when she left my daddy to try and make a better life for her and us, so she moved back to her hometown, Durham, North Carolina. However, the biggest problem was that she had no viable working skills other than working in corn and tobacco fields. Also, when she left, she could not take us with her. Her plan was to go back home and try and make a living for herself and come back and get us.

Our caretaker during this transitional period in her life was her sister who was married to my daddy's brother. It was three years from the time my mother dropped us off at her sister's house until we were able to join her as a family again. These three years were some of the darkest times in my family life. We endured so much physical and psychological abuse during these years.

But when I was finally united with my mother, I was so happy. I can remember the day like it was yesterday. I was sitting in the backseat of my uncle's car as he was taking me to be with my mother after those three years. The plan was to take the three youngest children first (me, my brother Jimmy, and my sister Rosa) and then on another trip take the other four.

Sitting in the backseat of the car, eight years old, all I could say over and over in my mind, "I am going home to be with my mama." So much joy was in my heart that day. Truly, I can remember it like it was yesterday, and I am now fifty-five years old. Such overwhelming joy filled my heart. But I did not know life could be bad being with someone who loved you, and you loved them back. I had no idea what life was going to be like when I got back with my mother, but I did not expect to live in the kind of substandard living I was about to endure.

Because my mother had little education, the only job she could find was being a cook at "greasy spoon" places and cafeterias. If all of our utilities were on at the same time, it was a miracle. I remember having to fill the bathtub up with water because the water was getting ready to be cut off. For nine years, survival was our main focus.

From day to day, we did not know how we were going to make it. My mother would cook a whole bag of rice just to feed us. Beans (Great Northern, pinto, black-eyed pea) were a stapled food in our house. Anything that would expand and increase, my mother cooked it. The favorite thing we loved for our mother to cook was homemade biscuits. She could cook some biscuits. They would be so soft and evenly brown on the top and bottom. Life was always about making it through the day, and the days were extremely long especially during the school year for me.

When you grow up in an impoverished environment, I think it is a given having good clothes to wear would be a constant problem. So sometimes I would go to school with mismatched clothes on. Of course, wearing garments like this to school often caused you to be the joke of the class. When this would happen to me, I would play it off, but I would be dying inside. I often tell people my self-esteem was so low by the time I was an adult that I did not know how to be "normal"—whatever that means.

Life growing up in poverty was awful! The fear of being laughed at in school dangled over my head every day of my life during the school year. But I got through each year, passing from one grade to another until I reach the twelfth grade. Oh, and by the way, I had only had one sibling that had finish high school, and that was my sister Rosa; she was two years ahead of me. All my other brothers and sisters (five) dropped out of high school.

In my twelfth grade, I was looking forward to graduating like my sister Rosa. We were somewhat close, but because she was two years older than me, she was blessed to have friends in our neighborhood, whereby their parents were educated and they had a better lifestyle than us. We know today this saved my sister from being a high school dropout because they gave her a vision for what life could be like if she finished high school and perhaps go to college.

Unfortunately, I did not have friends like this, so survival was still my mind-set. So going to school was what I supposed to do, but I really didn't know why I needed to go to school. I had no one in my life to bring clarity to this matter. The world was such a mystery to me.

Entering the last year of high school, I was just trying to survive. However, I had started working, so I was able to buy a few pieces of garments that were appropriate for school. I felt good about this, but the twelfth grade was "no piece of cake." What I realized after flunking the first semester in English, I had to pass the second semester to graduate from high school. I never thought about how important English was until I was faced with this dilemma.

I took a creative writing course the second semester, hoping this would be easy, and I would pass the class with no problem. After starting the class, I felt like I had gotten out of the frying pan and into the fire when the teacher began to teach the class. I knew immediately I was in trouble. I was not sure what this class was going to be like, but certainly, I had no idea I would be writing stories. This class was a nightmare! My mind could not put a subject and a verb together, nor did I have an understanding of punctuation. I did not know how to construct or stop a sentence. I really worked hard to try and make sense out of writing, but all I knew how to write was a run-on sentence. I had to pass this class in order to graduate from high school.

I don't think I never made a passing grade on any of my writings in this class. No matter how hard I worked, English just didn't make sense to me. But the whole while I was struggling in this class, not graduating from high school was constantly dangling over my head. I felt so ashamed and embarrassed. I wanted to fix it, but I felt powerless. I told no one.

So when the semester ended, which was the end of the school year, I did not know what to do. I was scared, and I definitely did not want to see my grade because I did not want to see that I had failed. Because if I did, this meant facing up to another truth: I will not be graduating, which I knew I was not capable of doing. My solution: never ask the teacher if I passed or not. To this day, I never knew my final grade in this class.

However, the hardest thing for me was going through the motion with my mother and sister acting as though I knew for sure I was going to graduate. Somehow my mother scraped up enough money to pay for my cap and grown, so everything was taken care of for my graduation. All the while this was going on, I was been haunted by the fact I might not graduate.

The school year ended, and graduation day arrived. I was one scared chick. All day long, internally I was in turmoil. I am sure I had created some story just in case my name was not called, so as my mother and my sister Rosa sat on the bleachers with me, I was praying hard inside.

When it was our time for our row to line up to receive our high school diploma, I got in line with everyone else. When I reached the stage and they called my name, while I wanted to be joyful, all I could feel was relief. So I plastered a smile on my face and went back to my seat and hugged my mother and sister. Even though I had received my diploma, I still felt like an imposter. I was so guilt-written that I never really experienced the joy of that day. I knew what was going on. It was the fact that I had a secret, and I was too embarrassed to tell anyone. I guess I did not want to be a failure.

This was such a conflict in my heart that I kept this secret for about twenty-eight years before the Lord allowed me to share it with anyone. But when He did, it was a period in my life that He could get the glory out of my situation. You see, by the time the Lord allowed me to share my story, I was then an owner of a writer's agency, Jabez Books. For five years, God had allowed me to become a published author, whereby I published and copyrighted personally over eight books. In 2014, I have written and published over twenty books. I will probably be releasing three to four more books in 2015.

When I think about my life and what I went through and where I am now, I realized my main debilitating problem was my environment. Was it nature or nurture? For me, it was nature—that which I grew up in defined and hindered my learning process. When you have a survival mind-set as a child, your focus and thoughts are on just making it day by day, especially when your parents have little education and they really don't know the impact of being educated. This was my situation. Because my mother had little education, she could not mentor me in this area. All she knew, I was supposed to go to school.

But I thank God today for His restoring grace. He restored to me the years that the cankerworm and palmerworm stole from me according to Joel 2. If we would allow Him to lead and guide us, we can never go wrong.

My biggest change came in my life when God allowed me to work for a library system. Surrounded by books, God began speaking to my heart about the importance of reading. I was a part of the Circulation Department, and one day, He spoke to my heart something to this effect: "Why do you think all these people are checking out all these books? It must be something to books." All the "bells and whistles" went off inside me. I immediately started checking out twenty-five to thirty books at a time. I had a thirst to read that could not be quenched.

I try to drive and read. Every break or lunch I got, I read books. I read all types of books: fiction and nonfiction (cooking, personal finance, self-help, organization, motivational, mystery, etc.). It was amazing what I found out in books. I felt like I had tapped into a resource that was never ending. To this day, I am an avid reader.

So not only do we own a writer's agency, but we also have five other departments under our consultant group. We have a PR and marketing firm, a management and entertainment service, a leadership institute, an event planning department, and a corporate training and coaching service.

God has truly blessed the fruit of my labor, and that little poor girl that I was is far from that poor little girl today. And because of all the things the Lord has allowed me to do and all the people He has allowed me to meet, I am convinced more than ever that the sky is no longer the limit for me. The universe is my goal and my classroom. Every day I wake up, I go to school. There are things I have never seen, and there are things I don't know. Therefore, I cannot afford to waste moments in my life. There are people who say things like, "Child, I am just killing time or wasting time." Two things I don't do: I don't kill time, nor do I waste time. Time is something we can never get back. We have to be productive citizens on this earth and maximize our existence.

What do you want to do in life? What do you want to be in life? Whatever your answers to these questions, I want you to know, you have no limitations. All you have is an access problem.

As I close this chapter, I want you to know that in order for you to thrive on this earth, you have to take on the mind-set of a global solutionist. While there might be a problem, but God has provided a solution for the problem. And if you would become one with the Father in prayer, He can download the solution to the problem within you.

I have a book out that I am on tour with that is called, "Pray & Grow Richer." For four years, I soaked and seek in the presence for about 80% of my time. I limited my comings and goings because I wanted a change in my financial portfolio. I read only books by Christian millionaires, and I did numerous thing to provoke the presence of God in my life for increase.

In four years, my income increased three times, created business ideas were stimulated, and God even taught me how to do graphic design and all types of technical programs. It was phenomenal. This year, we are preparing for the overflow even the more. We have already hired four other contract service providers to assist us with our anticipated growth in 2015, and we will be opening up a couple of businesses also in 2015.

We expect this to be a banner year for us and our company. We are big thinkers because we know, no matter where you begin in, life is certainly not the end of the matter.

So many people are prisoners to their past, but they don't have to be. You can create the world you desire by being the change you want to see. If you don't know how to do it, read up on it. If you don't know who to talk to, read up on it. If you don't know how to get the money you need, read up on it. Reading is an empowerment tool.

When I was writing my book, Pray & Grow Richer, I was led to write a whole chapter about reading; it was called, "The Empowered Mind." Here is an excerpt out of this chapter:

It is said that in five years you will be the same person, except for the CDs you listen to, the DVDs you watch, the books you read, and the people you hang around. If you want your world to change, you have to start reading TODAY!

It is also said: "If you read thirty to sixty minutes a day in a subject of your choice, after three years you will be known in your community, five years you will be known across the country, and after seven years, you will have worldwide recognition."

Listen, if you are in the body of Christ today and you are not a reader, you need to stop what you are doing and pray and ask God to give you the passion and the desire to read. Reading is extremely important to your mental, physical, emotional, and financial makeup. According to Myron Golden in his book, From Trash Man to Cash Man, "Rich people educate themselves, and poor people entertain themselves." This statement alone should provoke you to read if you are not a reader.

Reading provides greater avenues or more opportunities for God to expand you ministry sphere and financial portfolio.

Reading brings about expansion, and expansion brings about exposure.

Let's give God something more to work with.

I challenge you to wake up every morning expecting the universe to be in your favor. You are well able to abound, and there is nothing impossible for you to overcome. You are enough. You are smart enough. You are wise enough. You are clever enough. You are resourceful enough. You have enough ideas to pull off miracles. I expect great things out of you . . . Look out, world, here I come.

# Part 3

## I Can Read

Dr. Jamal Randy Allen Rasheed

The Lord himself goes before you and will be
with you; he will never leave you nor forsake
you. Do not be afraid; do not be discouraged.
(Deuteronomy 31:8)

# "In the Name of Thy Lord, Read."

Dr. Jamal Rasheed

*T*o many African American boys, reading is a curse and a curse word, as it was with Randy Allen. It comes with punishment, whooping, embarrassment, withdrawal of privileges, and sometimes even having your meals taken. Parents sometimes know not what we do until the damage is done, but the damage does not have to happen if you are a believer in God and you obey. Somehow or another, even believers skip over and misinterpret his word; and when the damage is done, we want to know why. Children follow the lead of parents, and if our black boys find leadership outside the family and outside the books of God, and the books that God has provided, the results will continue to be the shattering social statistics we see among our black boys and our black men. Randy's mother was a believer, and his father was not, thus begins the story of a black boy who had no clue and took most of his life searching, and finally he found it and read.

Randy's parents, who he later found out were never legally married, migrated to the Southside of Chicago from Memphis along with his baby brother Rickey, and three half brothers in 1957. In 1958, after his mother and father got into a physical fight at Christmas, his mother left his father taking him and his brother with her. At four years old, Randy was told at that point: "You are now the man of the house, Mama's little man." To many black men, that may sound familiar. That, in all honesty, became his new focus. Starting kindergarten in 1959 at Kosminski Elementary School, all he could remember was "you are the man of the house and always take care of your brother."

Randy's mother, who was a high school graduate, placed emphasis on education and always wanted him to do our homework but never had time to help because she was working, and many times he was told to keep the door closed and watch his brother. By the time he was six years old, his mom had a girl, Olla May, to watch him and his brother. Olla May was about twelve years old and decided to play house with him and his brother. In the process, as mother and father do, she introduced him to sex. Unfortunately, his life changed and he became interested in girls and not in education. Every six months to a year, his mother and brother moved to a different apartment, and that's also how often he changed schools. The concentration was still more about taking care of his brother and watching the house while his mother was gone than education and reading. There was not a focus on reading. Anything and idle times became the devil's playground.

By 1963, while in the fourth grade, his mother decided that he and Rickey needed to be baptized and learn more about God and the Bible. Going to church and being focused at age nine is not ideal, and I would not recommend any parent does that unless you personally provide the lesson.

Randy played most of the time in and out of church and spent the money, which was to go in the church plate, at the candy store along the way. He went to Bible school where he was not taught to read the word; it was read to him. This is where we are supposed to get our guidance, but the teacher must have missed. Joshua 1:8 says, "This book of the law shall not depart out of thy mouth; but thou shalt meditate therein day and night, that thou mayest observe to do according to all that is written therein: for then thou shalt make thy way prosperous, and then thou shalt have good success." He did not get to read what was written, so how would he know? Muslim children begin as early as four years old to read, recite, and memorize the Holy Quran from cover to cover.

By the time Randy was nine years old, he had ran away from home twice, been arrested for burglary and theft half a dozen times and by twelve, in a gang. His influences were not people who read. Black men in his age that were looked up to had money, clothes, women, and nice cars like Cadillacs. The system was graduating students through social promotion, and the church did not ask if you know how to read as long as you followed the instruction according to the word they read.

In 1966, his mother married, and they left Chicago for Flint, Michigan. That was supposed to be a better life. He lived across the street from Calvary Baptist Church, and despite the proximity, and he went to Sunday school and church more often, it did little to change his personality. They read bible stories to him just like everyone else. There was no emphasis on learning it for themselves, just listen to what they read. If Psalms 119:18 said, "Open thou mine eyes, that I may behold wondrous things out of thy law," the Sunday school teacher did not understand. Randy's eyes should have been reading. His stepfather worked for General Motors. He lived in a house, and for the first time, he went to school with white kids. That was a shock, and as they say, "You can take a Negro out of the country, but you can't take the country out of a Negro ." It proved to be the case with him in Flint. He brought his gangster ways with him. He even tried to start a gang in his school and teach his friends how to steal and break into the school at Bryant Junior High.

The priority was on getting you ready for Vietnam, working at General Motors or the AC Spark Plug company. The core courses were shop classes like metal shop, wood shop, and drafting. Most black boys dropped out at sixteen and went to the shops never to return to school. It was about getting a new Buick. Reading was for nerds and was not considered cool. He was not ready for that scene, and by eighth grade, his mother was sending him back to Chicago to live with his father. The other reason his mother sent him back to Chicago was because his stepfather and mother fought, and the last straw was when Randy went to the mattress and pulled out the gun.

It was now September of 1967, and Randy was back in Chicago living with his father. It needs to be said that all the years in between, his father was never absent; his mother just tried to keep him out of his life and would say bad things about him as a father. December of 1966, he sold his bicycle to the pawnshop to buy a train ticket back to Chicago to visit his father because his mother said if he wanted to see him, he would have to pay his own way. His father was just as persistent to keep communication. Randy feared his father, and it was not because he ever did anything to him; it was what he would do to him if he did get into any trouble according to his older brothers. Three different personalities begin to take shape in his life during this time, all from the different type people his half brothers were. Randy never differentiated between them, and his father preferred they saw each other as natural brothers. However, Randy's brother Edwin, or as he was called Ebbie, was different. He was the second of his father's first three boys. With Randy and his brother, there were five boys.

George Jr. was very intelligent, very well read, and smart in the field of electronics. However, he was a great thief, slick in every way and could talk his way out of anything. George taught Randy how not to have fear and how to fight. He was in a couple of gangs for survival, spent some time in the reform school as they call it in Illinois. He taught him how to survive legally and illegally, be smart, be street-smart, and be slick.

One day, an older bully in the neighborhood, who did not know George Jr. was his brother, hit him in the face and took his portable radio/record player. Randy told George Jr., and he had his friend find the guy. George brought him back with about ten of the guy's friends watching, made Randy hit the guy in the jaw as many times as he wanted to, and take his radio back. From that day on, he and his friends never bullied

Randy again. After a short term in the navy, George Jr. came back to Chicago, kept getting in and out of trouble. George Jr. spent most of his adult life in and out of state jails between Memphis and Chicago until he died of a drug overdose in 1991. He was working on two masters degrees at the time.

Ebbie introduced Randy to the world of music and fun. He learned to read music, not books because the popular thing in his neighborhood was singing as well. Ebbie taught him how to play the bass guitar, and he had a six-string guitar. It led Randy to joining the choir in high school and playing in the talent shows and taverns around the neighborhood. His neighborhood produced the Staple Singers, The Chi-Lites, Curtis Mayfield, and Ebbie traveled with The Five Stairsteps who also lived in our neighborhood to name a few.

When he got back to Chicago, Ebbie had been drafted and would shortly leave for Vietnam as a paratrooper. He was a happy person, but if you made him mad, then it was like Dr. Jekyll and Mr. Hyde. Edwin was the first to actually graduate from high school, and Randy wanted to graduate from the same high school he did, John M. Harlan High School.

Ebbie spent a lot of time with Randy and his younger brother Rickey from infant to twelve years old and reminded us that our mother told him to always take care of us, and he did when he could. He would visit Randy on weekends and sometimes spend the night when we lived on the other side of the city. Michael and George Jr. did not consider Randy and his brother and would get into it with Ebbie about the subject.

Today Ebbie reminds him he is keeping his promise to their late mother who died of cancer in October 1972, four months after my high school graduation. Ebbie is well versed with the Bible and has read the Quran from cover to cover, and we talk regularly about church, Islam, and spiritual direction. He is currently in and out of the veterans' hospital for posttraumatic syndrome and other physiological and physical damages the Vietnam War did to him.

Finally, Randy's other brother Michael was actually at the house with him when he returned to Chicago until he got drafted in 1968 and sent to Germany. Michael's influence was reading, dressing well, and women. He was considered to be the business intellect of the family. He was the go-to person regarding business and particularly finances. He was the organizer-leader type, and every organization he belonged to, he was the president. Michael said, "This family does not produce followers. We produce leaders." When Randy came back to Chicago, he had a hobby building model cars and racing HO cars. Michael said he was wasting time and my money. He found him a job at Mrs. Goines Cleaners in the neighborhood and strongly encouraged him to get rid of the toys and buying clothes because women like to see men dressed sharply.

Randy's dad was known for his choice of clothes as well. Michael would give him Italian-knit sweaters he could no longer wear, and Randy would go get a pair of dress pants to match. Michael also had a streak of militancy in him and started reading him Muhammad Speaks's *Message to the Black Man* and *The Black Panther* newspaper. His way to get Randy to read was by giving him something interesting and informative about what was going on with black people. His words were "in order to be a black leader, you have to understand who you are as black people." By 1969, Michael was gone to Germany, and I was left alone again.

By 1970, Randy was tired of and frustrated with gang banging, and his influence and reading began to revolve around the Black Panther Party in Chicago. Instead of fighting and killing brothers on the street about neighborhood, turf, and boundaries in a city that did not belong to them, he turned to the revolution of saving black people. Randy had read all the papers, listen to Bro. Fred Hampton, Mark Clark, Huey P. Newton, Bobbie Seal, Eldridge Cleaver, and now he could go all over the city because no one messes with the Panthers. They were neutral. Coupled with listening to the Honorable Elijah Muhammad and reading Muhammad Speaks, he joined the Afro History Club at his high school, and the advisor, Mrs. Linda Lane, introduced and encouraged us to read *Black Voices* which introduced him to the works of Langston Hughes, Richard Wright, Ralph Ellison, Frederick Douglas, LeRoi Jones (Amiri Baraka), Gwendolyn Brooks, Margret Walker, and the list goes on. It was by no coincidence that in 1970 he met his friend Norman Jones, even though they were from two different worlds.

Norman had graduated from Fenger High School in Chicago, a year ahead of Randy, and was attending Northern Illinois University. Norman and Randy had worked as stock clerks at a store, and he went on to get a job at Heinz drugstore before graduating. When the grocery store began to lay off workers because of the union and protest by Jesse Jackson, Norman got him a job at the drugstore as a stock clerk. Norman worked in the pharmacy and read a lot because he wanted to be a doctor. He left for college in the fall of 1971, and we kept in touch. They had two totally different lifestyles. Norman grew up with both parents, never got arrested, got into any problems at school, never got into or involved with any of those things that plague black boys growing up in Chicago. On the other hand, I was totally opposite.

The boy named Randy Allen who, while in eighth grade at Burnside Elementary School, was told by a teacher he would not amount to anything, was gang banger, and would end up dead or in prison. He was about to change. He graduated from eighth grade reading at a fourth grade level and had a fourth grade math score. He would turn a corner. Even though he would graduate from high school, he would meet Norman Jones who would invite him to spend a weekend with him at college, show him "a different world", and take him to an Alpha Phi Alpha Fraternity, Inc. and an interest meeting at Epsilon Phi Chapter.

It was then this evolution occurred. The step show by the Alpha's impressed him at that age; however, it was the "smoker" or the information meeting that took Randy afterward that impressed him more. He was surrounded by educated men who talked about all the famous men he had read or heard about: Dr. Martin Luther King Jr., Thurmond Marshall, Adam Clayton Powell, and the list goes on. The fact is that they were all Alphas and that I too could have the opportunity to be among those men. The catch: you have to have a 3.0 grade point average, and to get that, you have to read and study. They would take nothing less. The mission was clear, and the Alphas had given this high school student revolutionary new marching order. He never wanted to be a part of something as much as he would now crave to belong to this group of men.

Upon his return to school, he began to read more. In 1972, he graduated from Harlan with a 1.6 grade point average; and with the help of Alpha members at Northern Illinois University, he was able to get accepted through the CHANCE Program. Most of them were administrators and counselors in that program. On his first semester at Northern Illinois University, he had a 3.2 grade point average and pledged his second semester. While pledging, he had to learn such poems as "Invictus", "Test of a Man", "House of Alpha", "If", "The Man Who Thinks He Can" without respect to who wrote these poems. The words were powerful and strong they influence you and others. He had to read the history of Alpha Phi Alpha, all while keeping his grades as required. Alphas taught him, in the name of thou Lord, the importance of reading and why it was important to understand what you are reading and comprehending. They taught him how to breakdown what I was reading and how to interject it into his life and motivate himself to succeed. I must say the methods were nontraditional and would not be recommended for teaching purposes.

Randy Allen was not looking for a "role model." He was looking to survive, and God had a plan. Randy let go and let God as he endured life's numerous bumps and blows. Randy kept the faith as God spared him from drowning three times in his life and spared him from a bullet several times. God had his angels watching Randy, this lost child who had no earthly parental direction which could have come from the power of learning to read.

Randy knew his father in heaven would bring him through. God knew somebody would forget Psalms 119:105: Thy word [is] a lamp unto my feet, and a light unto my path; Matthew 4:4: But he answered and said, "It is written. Man shall not live by bread alone, but by every word that proceeded out of the mouth of God; Romans 15:4: For whatsoever things were written aforetime were written for our learning, that we through patience and comfort of the scriptures might have hope; II Timothy 2:7: Consider what I say; and the Lord give thee understanding in all things; I Timothy 4:13: Till I come, give attendance to reading, to exhortation, to doctrine. Somebody forgot that in the Holy Quran, it says: "Proclaim! (or read!) in the name of thy Lord and Cherisher, Who created all things."

Randy Allen did not forget who brought him a mighty long way because Randy is now Jamal Randy Allen Rasheed, God's child who went from reading four levels behind in eighth grade with a 1.6 grade point average in high school to earn a PhD. He has educated and saved over sixty thousand men from dying of prostate cancer, and is a fifteen year prostate cancer survivor He is a teacher and a sociologist. Most of all, he is an obedient child of God.

Several questions come to mind which could have saved Randy early, and I pose them to the reader. How often do you read to your son? How often does your son read to you? Who spends the most time with your sons? Are you allowing your son's father full and unlimited access and opportunity to raise him? How much time does your son watch television and play video games instead of having stimulating conversation about a book? Do you teach your son the importance of black history and his role? Do you point out the real black leaders other than football, basketball, movie, and rap stars? Do you read and have your son read to you the book of your faith?

All the above questions challenge a young black boy to look for love in all the wrong places, and he will choose to if he does not get it from home and from other responsible men. The answers and where he should begin to look is in the written words of our heavenly Father who has commanded him to read. Then he should reach out to his father and other strong male figures in his family. All books of God demand you to read, write, and recite. Randy Allen is now Jamal Randy Allen Rasheed, PhD, and Norman Jones is now Norman E. Jones, MD. What they have in common and what brought the two worlds together once were friendship, Alpha Phi Alpha Fraternity, and in the name of thy Lord who created man from a clot they read and obey God's holy ordinance to read.

Dr. Jamal R.A. Rasheed can be contacted by e-mail -jamal5@ sbcglobal.net

# Part 4

## Women Rule the World

*Ms. Katrina Ferguson*

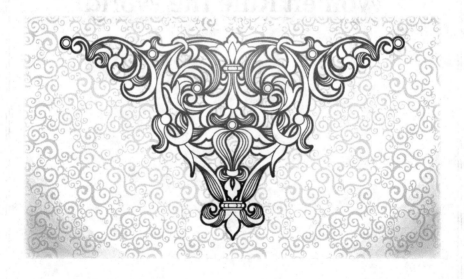

For we are his workmanship, created in Christ Jesus unto good works, which God hath before ordained that we should walk in them.

Ephesians 2:1

"Always remember, if your WHY is BIG enough, The HOW will take care of itself."

*Katrina Ferguson*

*H*ot does not even begin to describe the weather on this particular Independence Day. The sweltering heat of July was thick and muggy. The dense humidity felt as if you were walking through a steam room or maybe even the jungle. As heavy as the air was, her heart was heavier. At the time, her children were fifteen, fourteen, and seven years of age. Although she faced one of the most difficult seasons of her life, she had done a good job of hiding her pain. Putting on a positive face was important since her daughters looked up to her for strength, guidance, and motherly wisdom. *Independence Day . . . how ironic.*

That particular day, the drive home seemed longer than normal, as every stop light seemed perfectly timed to prevent her from reaching their home. Road construction seemed to pop up instantaneously. This holiday was not as joyous as some of the others had been not because of the meaning of Independence Day but because of the direction her life seemed to be going. The sky darkened long before dusk as storm clouds blotted out the sun and put a slight chill in the air. As suddenly as the temperature dropped, so did the rain . . . and her tears. Her oldest daughter noticed but did not dare to ask why her mother wept. She was old enough to pick up on the context clues and realized that life as they knew it was about to change. *Independence Day . . . how ironic.*

"What's wrong, Mommy?" asked the seven-year-old.

"Just sit back and play with your doll," said the oldest.

"But Mommy is crying," she exclaimed.

"I'm fine, baby. I'm fine," said the mother in an effort to console her child.

The closer they got to the family home, the more her heart rate increased. By the time she finally pulled into the long driveway, she was on the verge of hyperventilating. God seemed to be sending down rain with fury as the large, heavy raindrops pounded against the windshield with the same speed and intensity of the tears leaving her eyes. Her thoughts raced like the winds of the storms. There were to be no fireworks on this day, at least none in the skies. The storm made sure of that. *Independence Day . . . how ironic.*

The goal was to celebrate fifty years of marriage with him. As she sat there sobbing outside their home, she knew that would not be their reality. There is a saying that time will either promote you or expose you. That not only goes for people; it also goes for relationships. She tried. Really she did. Irreconcilable differences are . . . well . . . irreconcilable. There were only two real choices. She could continue down this dead-end street, unhappy and unfulfilled, risking her self-confidence while nullifying every lesson she had taught her girls about what a relationship built on love and trust should look like, or she could leave the relationship and hope for a do over.

In spite of having biblical grounds for divorce, she never intended to leave. She had done everything *she* could to make it work. She fasted, prayed, and sought counseling . . . everything. That Fourth of July, she learned a lesson that would follow her for the rest of her life. The lesson was although God answers prayers, He would never go against the will of one man to answer the prayers of another. We all have a right to our own will. Our choice is between God's perfect will for our lives and His permitted will. All we can do is trust that whatever happens, God will use it for our good. *Independence Day . . . how ironic.*

You may be asking yourself how I know so much about how she felt in the midst of the challenges she faced. I know because I am the woman. This was one of the most difficult seasons in my life; consequently, it was also one of my most tremendous times of growth. We have all heard it, said that "if it does not kill you, it makes you stronger." This was a strength-building season in my life. The days, weeks, months, and years to follow would present many other challenges that would strengthen me as well. These seasons are just moments of time, in time. Keeping in mind that these seasons do not last forever, just as winter does not; we will go through them more gracefully. Just remember, the seasons come, and they pass. In actuality, they came to pass.

Through all the challenging seasons of my life, I discovered a foundational truth that serves as fertilizer to help you grow through *every* difficult situation. This information separates kings from paupers, the successful from the unsuccessful. This information can cause anyone to achieve the success that they desire. That piece of information is simply your *WHY*, getting an understanding of *WHY* you were created. A clearly defined *WHY* will help you know your God-breathed purpose. God had something specific in mind for every one of us before the beginning of time, a definitive problem for us to solve. Our journey through this life is to discover His purpose and plan for our lives and ultimately live it. Being clear about that purpose or *WHY* will serve as an anchor in the turbulent waters of our journey.

Knowing *WHY* you were created is more important than knowing your name. Your reasons for doing something come first. The answers come later. If you are clear about your *WHY*, then the path to success is easier to find and follow, even when it gets rough. Your *WHY* is to your life what fuel is to a rocket. It blasts you into the future, in the direction that *you* need to move in to obtain absolute fulfillment and success. The key freedom that we crave, freedom to do what we choose with our time and money will only become evident as we get crystal clear about *WHY* we were created in the first place.

Being clear on my *WHY* meant that as the challenges continued to come forward, I focused on finding a way through them without losing sight of who I was created to be. I have built all the success in my life around this principle and have taught others all around the world to do the same. What that means is this: if your "WHY" is big enough, if your "WHY" is strong enough, if your "WHY" is huge enough, then how to do that thing will take care of itself.

Unfortunately (or fortunately, depending on how you look at it), knowing your *WHY* does not mean that your journey to success will always be easy, just that it will be worth it. It means that what you are going through, you can actually grow through so that ultimately your greatness will show through. It is totally up to you. When you realize that your decision to pursue your *WHY* is greater than any of the circumstances of your life, you will take everything that happens in stride, simply as part of the process of your growth and development, and will work together with all the other circumstances of your life to bring you to your goal. Without a BIG WHY, small obstacles are seemingly insurmountable. With a big *WHY*, the large obstacles become *absolutely invisible*. What this means is "if your *WHY* is *big* enough, the *how's* will take care of themselves."

For me, my *WHY* was my kids. I have added to my *WHY*, but my family has always been the foundation that made me get out of bed and push toward my goals, even when I did not feel like doing so. As I grew through what I was going through (a success tip), I began to look at how and WHY I was created and what it was that God wanted from my life. I studied the Bible to determine who I was in Christ, since the creator of a thing is the best resource for information about how the thing works or should work. Dr. Myles Munroe says that "if you don't know the use of a thing, abuse is inevitable." In the process of finding my purpose, there were several "WHY" Wisdom Keys that helped me along the journey. Those keys are being discussed in my new book that is being released in the Spring; in the meantime, here are several of the keys discussed there. Prayerfully, they will help you as well.

**"WHY" Wisdom Key No. 1:** *Successful people have a BIG WHY that causes them to do what is necessary, even when they do not feel like it.*

When I speak of successful people, I am speaking of success on your own terms; however, it is that you measure success. Even after the breakup of my family, I have continued to have my fair share of challenges and opportunities for growth. Through it all, I have kept my *WHY* in front of me. Of course, as the kids grew and their needs changed, so did my *WHY*. One of the most popular acronyms for the word *WHY* is "What Hurts You?" In other words, what touches you so deeply that it makes you cry to think about not achieving it? What is the problem that you were created to solve, the problem that moves you at the core of your being? What gives you pain in the pit of your stomach or a lump in your throat when you think about disappointing those waiting for you to get yourself together and live your destiny?

For some people, those emotions stop them rather than driving them enough to make things happen. For the successful person, this becomes their motivation to keep going. As an alternative acronym for WHY, try "What Helps You?" What helps you get out of bed early and stay up late working toward your goals? What helps you go the extra mile and do a better job than is expected? What helps you become more so that you can have more and do more? Choosing a faith-based WHY, rather than a fear-based WHY is a much more powerful position. Rather than being scared to action, you are moving forward in an inspired and enlightened state. Choose faith over fear.

**"WHY" Wisdom Key No. 2:** *Successful people use adversity as fuel to propel them to their goals.*

Many people use challenges and adversities as the reasons they cannot succeed. The reason that you think you cannot be successful should be the reason that you must be successful. For instance, many use their children as their excuse for not succeeding when their children should be the reason WHY they must succeed. My children were my *WHY* and a very *BIG WHY* at that. At first, it was all about survival. The bare necessities were my main priority since I had to do things on my own. The happy little family I had envisioned for myself was no more, and it was time for me to accept my season as a single parent and move toward my goals with speed and boldness. While balancing work, kids, activities, and church, I continued to look for a better way. Something about eating was important to them, so I had to figure out a way to feed them.

Living just above the poverty level did not sit well with me. Knowing that God had a bigger plan for my life, I set out to find out what it was while providing for my children and doing what was necessary to create a life for us all.

**"WHY" Wisdom Key No. 3:** *Successful people do what they have to do now so that ultimately, they can do what they want to do.*

Up until the separation, I was a stay-at-home mom. Our house was the Kool-Aid house where my kids' friends came to play. As a result of the shift in my life, I had to do something to meet our basic needs. Even though I had great aspirations of becoming a successful businessperson, I had to start somewhere so that we were not hungry. A job became a starting place to solve our problems. Boy was I glad that my start did not dictate my finish. The job was an okay place to start, but I knew it was not where I was going to finish. Walking into a building every day that did not have my name on it, being paid what someone else said I was worth, working when they told me to work, taking off when they permitted me to do so meant I was building someone else's dream while my dream lay dormant. My *WHY* was the key to me pursuing my dream of becoming a successful business owner, featured in magazines, and rubbing shoulders with some of the most prolific minds and speakers of our time.

**"WHY" Wisdom Key No. 4:** *Successful people never ever give up on their dreams, yet they do separate themselves from negative thinking, people, and habits.*

People sometimes look at my life now and think that it was easy for me. The houses, cars, vacations, and multiple streams of income—they all came with a price. There have been many more businesses fail than have been successful. Part of the process is to learn from what does not work so that you do not continually make errors in judgment. Additionally, you cannot allow your past to dictate your future. It is so easy to have pity parties when things are not going your way.

That Fourth of July, I could have simply given up on life. I could have settled for a meager existence and been on welfare for the rest of my life. Please do not misunderstand; I am not saying that public assistance is a bad thing. You would be surprised at the number of successful people in the world that have had to get help in order to survive at some point in their lives. When it becomes a way of life, however, and you are given money and resources without having to work for them, it can negatively affect your mental well-being, your self-esteem, and your confidence. The programs were designed to assist the public during challenging financial seasons, not as a way of life.

My grandmother said, "A closed mouth does not get fed." Do not be too proud to get the help you need in the season that you need it. Just do not allow it to become the crutch that dulls your intellect and kills your drive. Pride often keeps us from allowing others to help us. Scripture says that "pride goes before destruction." Use the help to position yourself to help others. Charity is a two-way street. Moreover, if you find yourself falling, as my good friend Les Brown always says, "Fall on your back because if you can look up, you can get up."

**"WHY" Wisdom Key No. 5:** *Successful people distract themselves from their distractions.*

Obstacles are what you see when you take your eyes off your goal. Any obstacle that stands in the way of your moving toward your goal is a distraction. Most of the time, distractions are neither good nor bad; they tend to be things, habits, or people that we consistently allow to interfere with our forward movement. Successful people distract themselves from their distractions. There is always a way to achieve your goals and dreams! Find it. If you cannot find it, make it. Continue moving forward at all costs; your *WHY* depends on it.

Yes, what you love is a clue to your purpose and your destiny. It is also a clue to where you will find your greatest resistance. Expect it. Often our way through the distractions of our lives is about reevaluating what we are giving priority status in our lives. Some relationships, some jobs, social media, even our children can be distracting us from who God intended us to be and who He intended for us to bless. Some of us need to cut the information umbilical cord and turn off the television and the Internet. Watching television takes you out of your own life and into someone else's. One of my mentors calls television the electronic income reducer. Stop watching others tell you their vision and work on your own. Remember, focus is crucial to our process, and what we focus on expands. No matter what goes on around us, we have to give it minimal attention so that we keep our goal destination in sight.

It is very difficult for me to give you everything you need in life to be prosperous in this short chapter. Success comes from a combination of thoughts and actions. What I do know for sure is that knowing your *WHY*—your reason for being—is one of the most important variables for your success. There has to be a strong enough reason *WHY* you want to succeed. There has to be something that gives you the necessary energy to keep going when all the odds are against you. We all have one thing in common: a *BIG WHY* will move you in the directions that will bring fulfillment into your life and the lives of others that you touch through your actions. Whatever you do, find your *WHY* and fly. Live a life so powerful that people will want to read your story and point to you as an example of greatness!

## EXERCISE

Have you figured out your *WHY?* If you were already clear on your *WHY,* maybe it's time to renew it. Write yourself a letter. Start it by saying how much you love yourself; we do not tell ourselves that enough. Then begin to write your *WHY.* Why do you need to be successful? Who are the people in your life that you have to become the best version of "you" to support? Is there something in your heart that keeps you awake at night dreaming of the possibilities for your life? Is there a cause that you can get behind and work toward to make the world a better place? Everybody reading this may have a different answer, yet we will all have a *WHY.* Once you have written the letter, put it somewhere where you can see it often. It will serve as a reminder and inspiration for you to stay the course of living on purpose and doing destiny.

If you would like to connect with me, send me your letter by e-mail to Katrina@KatrinaFerguson.com.

It would be my pleasure to offer you some assistance and a free tool that will assist you on your journey to becoming your greater self. Also, visit my website at www. KatrinaFerguson.com for even more resources to assist you.

# Part 5

## Surviving the Hard Times

## Ms. Teresa Ann Hailey

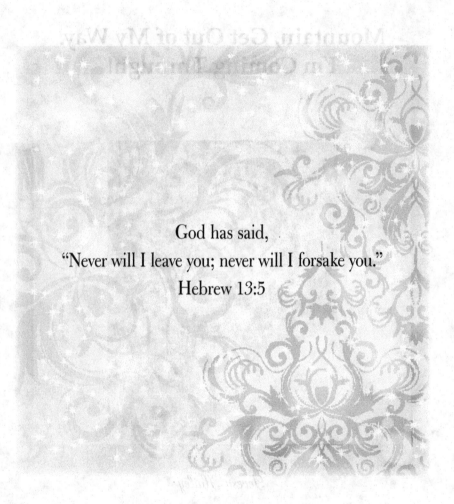

God has said,
"Never will I leave you; never will I forsake you."
Hebrew 13:5

# Mountain, Get Out of My Way.
# I'm Coming Through!

*Teresa Hailey*

*I* want to start my chapter with the word *responsibility*. Dictionary.com states the meaning as being responsible, answerable, or accountable for something within one's power, control, or management. Those are some powerful words. Each of us is responsible for ourselves. It is a fact that our actions and behaviors can affect someone else's emotional state of mind. It can also make a difference if someone lives a full and fruitful life or a damage life full of range, anger, hate, crime, and dismay.

In all our lives, we will experience some challenges. It took me a while to learn and understand that problems and situations make you a stronger, wiser, and better person. Regardless of what mountain is in your way, always try to figure out how to climb it.

Over the years, we all have heard both women and men come out and say that they were once a victim of sexual abuse. Too often I would hear my friends say, "What took them so long to say something? They must be lying or after money." I myself did not speak up because I was about six years old. I thought my babysitter sticking his penis in my mouth was normal.

My cousin and I would often talk about how a relative would force her to perform sexual acts. It did no good to tell anyone. I have learned that it is best to do and say nothing.

When you speak up, the abuser becomes the victim. You must have a witness or be able to catch that person on tape. If not, no one will believe you. I have discovered if the abuser is the leader in a family or well thought of, that person will always be believed over the victim. And if the abuser is a public person, you don't stand a chance of justice without a witness or catching that person on tape.

## "Mountain, Get Out of My Way. I'm Coming Through!"

Around 1979, myself, Mrs. Patrice Bean-Kane, who at the time was working at the Colorado Civil Rights Commission and about five other people started one of the first Martin Luther King march/parade in Denver, Colorado. I don't remember all the details, but I do remember all the problems it took getting organized and trying to get the public to participate. *Wow!* Look at the Denver, Colorado, march now. I believe it is the second largest march to Atlanta, Georgia. I look at it now and say I remember when we could not even get fifty people to participate. Now the participation is in the thousands.

I remember that local TV and radio stations would not play our public service announcement, or if they did, it was at some ungodly hour. I remember there were two marches/parades. Our group arrived at 11:00 a.m., and the second group arrived at noon. It was clear that the two groups did not get along. Our group had State Representative Wilma Webb who presented the bill in the state of Colorado to make Martin Luther King Jr.'s birthday a national holiday. We also invited Martin Luther King III to serve as our guest speaker. So truly our group had the leadership, contacts, etc.

I was very interested in the Civil Rights Movement, so after the Denver event, I spoke with Martin Luther King III after which I moved to Atlanta, Georgia.

One day, Martin III asked me if I would be interested in working for him being his assistant I said yes. What an opportunity. He made it **perfectly** clear to me, not to say anything to anyone, not even my parents because he had to first talk to his mother (Mrs. Coretta Scott King) and clear everything with her. Martin's office was also inside Mrs. King's office. When you arrive in Mrs. King's office, there was a sitting area which looked like a living room, and inside that area was about four small offices and Mrs. King's office.

At times I really felt out of place because most of the employees at the King Center came out of the Civil Rights Movement. They had marched, boycotted, went to jail, and were even beaten with Dr. King. Here I was, a dark-skinned middle-class black girl from Denver, Colorado, who I was told did not know how to get down. Many of the employees and people at SCLC felt that I had not paid my dues.

The waiting was killing me; a lot of times Martin was out of town, so I could not see or talk to him. I was close with one of the staff members, or so I thought. I felt it was okay to tell her. I was about to boost I had to talk to someone. At lunch one day, I told her. Later, I learned she was the last person that I should have said anything to. I did not know she had been trying to get promoted to Mrs. King's office for years. I, on the other hand, moved from Denver, Colorado, had never been a part of the Civil Rights Movement, and had not paid my dues. I repeatedly heard, "Why is she here? Where did she come from? She does not know how to get down."

She was mad, and she confronted Martin III about it. Needless to say, I was told that I was no longer going to be considered for the position. I cried for days. It was a big learning experience for me. My number one responsibility at the time was to say nothing. If I could not be trusted with something small, how could I be trusted with something big?

To be very honest, looking back, I was not ready for such a great opportunity or responsibility. I was a people pleaser, I talked too much, I was always some place I had no business being, and I was always into someone else's business.

Question/Quiz:

1. Name one event in your life that was life-changing.

_____

_____

_____

2. What did you learn from it?

_____

_____

_____

    I was working on Rev. Jesse Jackson's presidential campaign. One day, about six of us went to small towns and cities in Georgia educating and registering people to vote. We had been out in the hot sun for hours. When we returned back to our van, we were met by five Ku Klux Klan members dressed in full Klan regalia. Because of my leadership abilities and desire to stand up. Rev. Hosea Williams, who was once Dr. King's Field General and was on the balcony with Dr. Martin Luther King Jr. when he was shot and killed, asked me to travel and work for him.

Rev. Hosea Williams, Rev. Jesse Jackson,
Dr. Martin Luther King, Jr.
And Rev. David Ralph Abernathy

The position afforded me an opportunity to travel, meet a lot of people, and attend a lot different events. I was one of the people that helped get him elected while he was in jail. I also worked on his political bid for Congress.

### *"Mountain, Get Out of My way.*
### *I Am Coming Through!"*

I was blessed to be born and raised by my biological parents. Many adopted men and women cannot say that. Even through adoption is beautiful, there will come a day when the adopted family will tell the boy or girl that they have been raising, "We are not your real mother or father."

I have a cousin who was adopted. She was adopted by a very loving couple who made her feel like she was their own child. Later in life, she felt a void in her life. I often wonder how I would feel living each day not knowing the two people that were responsible for me being on this earth. Years ago, my cousin was successful at locating her two brothers; she learned that they have the same father yet different mothers. She was hit with a ton of bricks when she discovered that her father was a national recording artist Roy Hamilton.

Roy Hamilton was an American singer who achieved major success in the United States R&B and pop charts in the 1950s. He was best known for his recordings of "You'll Never Walk Alone", "Unchained Melody", and "You Can Have Her" *(Roy Hamilton.com)*. Her brothers and their families get together as often as possible. It brought so much joy to my life when she told me that she got in contact with both of her brothers. And the three families united. I was given the honor to witness the three families together. It was such a blessing. I think that adoption is beautiful for the women who cannot have children, a family that has a lot of love to give.

I feel that everyone must take their relationships, dating, love, sex, and marriage seriously. Your action can and will affect another human being's emotional state of mind and life. Ladies, I feel that we allow men to take advantage of us. Just because he says you are cute, he likes, or loves you does not give him the keys to your vagina. Your body is a precious jewel; treat it as such. Only certain people get to examine and touch the jewel. Too often we have sex with someone just because he is handsome, the type of car he drives, or his title. Now you are faced with a baby that you cannot afford or want. You cannot go after him for child support or hold him responsible because you don't even know his last name.

Now your parents are left to raise and care for your child, or the child becomes a part of the system going from foster home to foster home. It is so very important that we know our worth. You are a winner; you can do everything that you set your mind to. Develop your plan and then work it. Never settle for less, for you deserve nothing but the very best.

Question/Quiz:

1. When entering into a relationship, do you first start out being friends?

_____

_____

_____

2. Do you observe your potential mate/spouse?
A. Are they marriage material?
B. How do they treat their family?
C. Are they responsible?
D. Do you have the same financial goals?
E. Do you have the same family values/goals?

If your friendship/relationship is lacking communication or the above components, having casual sex is the last thing that you want to do. Being responsible is very important; it can make a difference in a child being born in a loving and caring home or becoming a part of the system.

I often say life is not fair. When I was in my late twenties, I was told that I had fibroid tumors. They started off with little or no side effect, and then as the years passed, they became very painful and grew to the size of a grapefruit. At the age of thirty-four, I was forced to have a hysterectomy. I had many talks with my doctor before the operation. I wanted so very much to be able to have children. Because of the results of my test, the doctor told me that he would do the best that he could to save my female organs so that one day I could bear a child. Needless to say, he was not able to, so one of my lifetime dreams and desires to be a mother was crushed. I still remember when he told me that I would never be able to give birth to a child and to look at adopting. I felt depressed, a sense of hopelessness, and less than a woman. I felt no man wants a woman that cannot bear his child.

I thought about adoption; I even checked into it. I wanted to be very responsible in my decision. I was not married, and it was and still is very important for me to raise a child with both a mother and father.

## "Mountain, Get Out of My Way. I'm Coming Through!"

I once lived next door to where I worked. One morning, the security officer came and got me. She advised me that the apartments that were located next door were on fire. I cannot even begin to tell you what it is like to see everything that you own burn. I and about ten other coworkers lost everything. I was homeless for about three days until the leasing office, along with the American Red Cross, was able to place me in another apartment. I thank God for the community, my Continental Airlines family, the director, my management team, and coworkers. They helped me and gave me so much. About ten days after the fire, I moved into a townhouse; I was given food, clothes, and furniture. I had more after the fire than before the fire.

I lost days of work; I had to get back into the groove of things. I put the fire behind me and moved forward. I really wish I could have sought help or talked about the fire, trying to forget about it and put it out of my mind was not the answer. Because I am paying for it today. I have learned that when you suffer any type of trauma, you have to pray about it, seek counseling, and have a very strong support system.

## "Mountain, Get Out of My Way. I'm Coming Through!"

I got over that mountain; I then started to fulfill my dream of becoming a homeowner. I wish I had help, I was looking with no help. I started reading every book that I could get my hands on. I attended every free workshop that was offered. I learned everything that I could about home ownership. I first had a meeting with a lender to see where I was, how much house I could afford, and what I needed to do to purchase my first house. It took me three years. The first year, I paid off all my bills; the second year, I saved my money, and the third year, I started looking. I must have looked at over thirty houses before I decided to build.

At the time I was working for Continental Airlines, and living in Houston, Texas. Management announced that our office would be moving to a new location closer to the airport. So I started looking at builders close to the new office.

I discovered a community that was only ten minutes from my job. When I first started looking, they had about thirty open lots. I kept praying; I still was not ready to sign a contract.

One day, the owner and president of the company was in town and in the office. The salesperson told him about me. After we laughed and talked, the owner told me, "I really appreciate your determination." There were only two lots left. One was the largest and the most expensive in the subdivision, and it carried a lot premium of $10,000. The other lots were either free or up to $5,000. The owner told me, "We are trying to close the community out. If you sign a contract right now, I will **give** you the $10,000.00 lot free of charge."

I called my real estate agent; she came flying over. I signed the contract, and my dream of home ownership was on the way. Everything went like clockwork. I watched the house being built, I took a lot of pictures, and I closed and moved in. After closing and signing all those papers, I got the key and went to the house. I thanked God all the way to the house.

Everything was going great, until one day, my real estate agent contacted me and reminded me that I had signed a two-year arm. I did not understand why I needed to do that because when I closed, I needed a 520 FICA score. I had a 750 FICA score. At that time, my mortgage payment was only $900 a month. When I closed on my new two-thousand-five-hundred-square-foot Home, the lot and upgrades came to $151,000. When I refinanced, I put up an additional $30,000 (cash). I felt so good because I knew my monthly payments and balance would go down. The loan officer told me there was a big problem but assured me that everything was being handled. I received my first statement; my monthly payment jumped from $900 a month to $2,100 a month. I called and went by the bank just about every day. I kept getting the run around.

After about one year, I received a letter telling me that I had been a victim of mortgage fraud. One day, I was watching the news on TV and saw the loan officer along with others being arrested, handcuffed, and placed in a police car. Over twenty people had been affected. I knew something was wrong, but I could not prove it. I received some money back, but nothing close to the $40,000 plus that I lost.

### *"Mountain, Get Out of My Way. I'm Coming Through!"*

Question:

1. When you closed on your house, signed for an apartment, or purchased your car, did a lawyer read your contract before you signed?

_____

_____

_____

2. Did you sign not really understanding what you signed?

_____

_____

_____

The average person signs a contract not really understanding what they are signing. And people don't read what they are signing. In most cases even if they read what they signed they still don't understand. We sign because we know if we want the item, service, etc., we must sign.

Please understand that regardless if you are purchasing a car, closing on a house, renting an apartment, or signing an agreement or any type of a contract, you have the right to have an attorney to read it first. Had I received my closing papers before I signed and had an attorney to review the contract, I would have never signed. Please understand that you have the right to have a lawyer review all contracts before you sign them. You may think a lawyer is too expensive, that is why I am now a member of Legalshield. My membership gives me access to a lawyer twenty-four hours a day and for only $19.95 a month. A lawyer will write letters, make phone calls, and review all my contracts. They have appeared in court with me and completed my living will and yes, for only $19.95 a month. Check out my Web site: www. legalshieldassociate.com/go/Teresa Hailey. To review what LegalShield has to offer.

### *"Mountain, Get Out of My Way. I'm Coming Through!"*

Just as I bounced back, my mother developed a cold that would never go away; as a matter of fact, it got worse. One Thanksgiving she was rushed to the hospital where we learned that she had fluid on her lungs. The doctors told us that she had stage four lung cancer, and there was nothing that they could do for her. She was sent home with less than six months to live. She passed two months after being diagnosed. I was in the bed next to my mother when she passed. That whole experience was life changing.

I turned the TV on, and every channel was announcing that Mrs. Coretta Scott King had passed. I did not know that she was sick. Friends and relatives from Atlanta started calling. They passed away hours within each other; they both died from cancer. My mother's funeral was on a Monday, and Mrs. King's was on a Tuesday.

The day of my mother's funeral, I noticed that some of her personal items were missing. I finished dealing with her funeral, and the next day, I hired an attorney. My mother died at 3:00 a.m. By twelve noon, a cousin had stolen just about everything of value. One brother held the other brother hostage; the police and SWAT was called. Things got really ugly and fast. Over $50,000 was spent on attorney's fees fighting in court to attain back what my mother wanted her children to have.

I became very depressed and was in a lot of pain. I knew that I needed help, so I got it. My therapist had me to read a book and advised me to be ready to talk about the book at our next meeting. When I started reading the book, I was shock because everything that I read in the book, I saw in my cousin. My therapist wanted me to read the book and to understand that I nor anyone else could change my cousin. I clearly understood that my cousin was a sociopath. A sociopath is a person that has the following characteristics:

## Manipulative and Conning

They never recognize the rights of others and see their self-serving behaviors as permissible. They appear to be charming yet are covertly hostile and domineering, seeing their victim as merely an instrument to be used. They may dominate and humiliate their victims.

## Pathological Lying

Has no problem lying coolly and easily, and it is almost impossible for them to be truthful on a consistent basis. Can create and get caught up in a complex belief about their own powers and abilities, and extremely convincing and even able to pass lie detector tests.

## Lack of Remorse, Shame or Guilt

A deep-seated rage, which is split off and repressed, is at their core. Does not see others around them as people but only as targets and opportunities. Instead of friends, they have victims and accomplices who end up as victims. The end always justifies the means, and they let nothing stand in their way.

## Callousness/Lack of Empathy

Unable to empathize with the pain of their victims, having only contempt for others' feelings of distress, and readily taking advantage of them.

## Irresponsibility/Unreliability

Not concerned about wrecking others' lives and dreams. Oblivious or indifferent to the devastation they cause. Does not accept blame themselves but blames others even for acts they obviously committed (Scott A Bonn PhD).

My therapist told me that there was no cure or medicine that could help. I have received phone calls from other victims that have expressed that my relative has stolen their life savings and has ruined their credit. Many were left penniless. Law enforcement cannot do one thing because he is skilled at what he does. He will steal from you, flip the switch and file a lawsuit against you, and take you to court.

It is because of this life-changing event that I am spending the rest of my life educating people about the importance of having a living will and a life insurance policy. Please protect yourself and your family. Too often I hear people say, "I don't have anything."

Please understand: everyone needs a living will and a life insurance policy. I have teamed up with a company called Legalshield. They provide the most affordable living will. They also offer much more. Check it out at www. legalshieldassociate.com/go/teresahailey. Protect your family today!

Question:

Do you have a living will?

_____

_____

_____

Do you have a life insurance policy?

_____

_____

_____

Does your life insurance policy have a cash value with it?

_____

_____

_____

If you have children under eighteen, are they protected if something happens to you? If not, they can become the ward of the state.

Too often people tell me that they are covered, and they are not. Please take the time to confirm what you have. If you have a life insurance policy with your job, do you know how much it is for?

My mother died in 2006; it is now 2015, and I am still in the midst of a legal battle. When death happens, it should bring a family closer together. There are too many families today that are not speaking because a family member did not have his or her "Life Events Plan" in order. Once again, responsibility, it is your responsibility to make sure that your last wishes are in order.

Please don't say, "It won't happen to me." My parents said the same thing. Call me today. Let's get your living will completed.

Be on the lookout for my next book. In the mean time, I would love to hear from you. E-mail me at shining stars_2015@yahoo.com.

For speaking engagements or information, please contact Teresa Hailey by e-mail: teresahailey@yahoo.com

## References

Bonn, Scott A., PhD 1/22/2014 - www.psychologytoday.com - How to Tell a Sociopath from a Psychopath.

# Part 6

## Being Adopted, My Feelings Matter

## Mr. Joshua Schuler

Praise be to the God and Father of our Lord Jesus Christ,
The Father of compassion and the God of all comfort,
Who comforts us in all our troubles, so that we can
Comfort those in any trouble with the comfort we
Ourselves have received from God.
II Corinthians 1:3-4

# I Define Who I am

*Mr. Joshua Schuler*

*T*o be born into this world is a gift. Every one of us that receives this gift of human form is automatically set apart from the many other life inhabitants on our planet. The fact that you can be reading this and consciously comprehending ideas, internalizing emotions, and flipping the page to read further is a wondrously human ability. Observe other life, whether plant or animal. The small bird calling at sunrise, the tiny ant rounding the toe of your shoe, the newly planted tree still being braced until its roots take fully into the ground—all are possible ways that you could have entered this world. Instead, you were gifted a body, mind, and soul—each interdependent of the other, each working in harmony to yield a person whom has the most unique of capabilities.

To be born is indeed a gift. It is God saying I have a plan, and you are playing a starring role in my greatest of productions "Life." We, of course, are not in the director's chair at time of birth. And because of this absence of choice, our lives can begin many differing ways. I could have been born in a small tribal village or maybe a sprawling modern city. I could be the only child born unto a widow who's recently lost her husband, to a royal family anxiously awaiting the throne's heir, or to a mother now unexpectedly pregnant after already bearing four children, not planning on a fifth child to raise and care for on a shoestring budget.

All and more are possible. Just as a farmer sows his seeds, there are infinite outcomes; yet based upon his understanding of the soil in which he's planting, the possible outcome is more defined. Sure there can be differing harvests from year to year. All the while, it is expected that the soil will do its part and produce. You see, the soil is where life takes root. It is the nourishment, the fertile womb that incubates and stores within it all potential. Our lives mirror this natural process. Once born, we are now the seed placed in the hands of caretakers. The guardians of this child provide all that is required for growth. They are the soil.

I received the greatest gift on January 10, 1986. Completely healthy, I had all the potential that any infant could ask for. Though as circumstances would have it, my single mother was unfit to be the soil God knew my life to need. Alcohol abuse and deepening mental instability had troubled her for some time before my arrival. I was to be her baby boy, the one that could possibly make right all the wrong her life had dealt up to then. It wouldn't be so.

Mere months after I was born, close family intervened, and I was placed within child services on route to a foster family. One foster family became two, and the course very well could have continued until one fateful day marked my life's course. It was a coworker of my foster mother, a dedicated police officer with circumstances of his own that left his wife unable to bear another child. Rested upon his heart was the image of a son, the son they were incapable of having naturally. He received word of me and quickly made arrangements for an initial visitation. My dad has always told me that the moment he saw me, he loved me. And after six months of system processing, I now had the designation of adopted child.

Through my early years, I understood adoption as simply meaning I was different. My parents were clear with me from the earliest of understanding. "You are adopted. You are our son," they would remind me. This greatly informed my sense of belonging and place. I felt intentionally loved and cared for. While particular circumstances were different from most other families, I rarely dwelled upon them. Some personal qualities highlighted these differences for others to remark upon once I was in grade school. One in particular was the physical difference between my parents and me. They were a fair-skinned Caucasian couple. I, on the other hand, have Eastern Indian blood from a biological father native to India. I've never met him, but I'd have to imagine he's fairly dark in skin complexion. My darker features were points of dissimilarity, but I quickly made them into distinctions.

One of my adoptive mother's favorite childhood stories involving this distinction is of me introducing myself to a new neighbor boy of my age. "Hi, my name is Joshua, and I'm Indian *beaming with pride*." "Hello, my name is Bryce, and I'm a Cowboy," responded my new neighbor friend.

My parents' openness about my adoption from the very beginning was a tremendous service to me. I didn't have to second-guess our dissimilar looks or even behavioral traits. There was no skeleton in the closet regarding my biological mother's situation. In fact, I had an open adoption that permitted her visitation with me for birthdays and holidays. All equated to me acquiring a depth of understanding into my life's journey in addition to an entire side of my biological family that could have been compromised if not for this transparency. I'm forever grateful to my parents for permitting this and to my biological family for reserving space in their lives and hearts for me to experience them fully.

Since my young adolescence, a lot has changed within my family. At age eight, my adoptive parents divorced after twenty-five years of marriage. At ten years of age, my dad remarried, and I acquired three older stepbrothers. With all these family dynamics in flux, it was the good soil that had me rooted during tough transitions. At twenty-nine years of age, I'm continually learning as the past informs my present and my present state of being informs my future.

Our differences in life circumstance can either become our building blocks for walls that separate us from others, or they can be embraced fully and incorporated into the whole of humanity, permitting us to live fully, love intentionally, prosper continually, and *shine!*

1. What is a defining trait you have that individualizes you?
2. What is a defining trait you have that is common?
3. How do you manage the experience of both in a way that permits you and others to shine?

# Part 7

## The Power of Family Unity

*Paula R. Bryant & Sarah E. Bryant*

We know that in all things God works for the
good of those who love him,
who have been called according to his purpose.
Romans 8:28

# Mother and daughter
# Bitter or Better?

*Paula and Sarah Bryant*

*I*t was the middle of winter in Sioux Falls, South Dakota, and we were both in transition. Rolling into the airport that frosty night in late February, first by airplane and then by wheelchair, was the beginning of a month-long experience that would test our relationship as mother, daughter, and friends. The good thing was that our relationship, having been proven through the years, was stronger than ever. But we were entering uncharted territory. We would soon have to face and overcome many challenges—working together, understanding each other, and above all, keeping our eyes on the big picture. This experience would definitely test whether we were going to become bitter or better.

As a freelance writer, editor, and editorial project manager, it wasn't difficult for me to flex my schedule and make the trip. I could easily clear a few days for travel and then juggle my time to help my daughter Sarah get situated in her new apartment in Chicago. But my role during this trip was minimized. I was in the process of coming through an illness that had shut me down for three months. As a result, I couldn't lift heavy weight; I had to eat a special diet and get plenty of rest, and I was taking several medications. So I told Sarah that I could help with packing and unpacking boxes and getting everything in the right places once we were in Chicago.

Sarah, on the other hand, had a more rigid schedule. She had less than a week, with minimal help, to get everything loaded into the moving truck, drive almost 575 miles to Chicago pulling her car on a tie dolly, handle details with her new leasing company, unpack the truck and car, and begin getting situated before starting a new, challenging job—all in absolutely freezing weather. Oh, and did I mention that she somehow had to be rested before she started work? Ha! As an added plus, we discovered upon arriving at her new apartment that commuter trains ran all day and most of the night just below her window.

Our first night was literally an adventure. Between the constant squeaky noises and flashing lights, trying to get just a few hours of unbroken sleep proved to be more than a challenge. So the day after we arrived, Sarah talked to her building management, and we moved out of the first apartment into the same unit three floors higher. Thankfully, a couple of her friends came and helped Sarah move everything from the seventh to the tenth floor, and that made getting rest possible . . . but what a whirlwind! We were definitely breaking ground in harsh new territory.

* * * * * * * * * * *

Using the term *harsh new territory* is putting it lightly. The move was both physically and emotionally exhausting. The physical, like my mom said, was moving from one state to the other in less than a week. There were no movers, and since my dad couldn't come, there were barely any men to help with heavy lifting. My mom and I were the primary players. But again, she couldn't do as much as she liked. She was dealing with several health issues.

When I first saw her, it was a sight I will never forget. I was waiting to pick her up at the airport in Sioux Falls. Instead of walking off the plane, she was being pushed in a wheelchair. This completely shattered me emotionally. She has always been my rock, so to see her frail and sick—she looked like she had lost at least fifty pounds—was shocking. But despite how she felt, she wouldn't miss this move for the world. I was leaving my first new producing job in Sioux Falls for a new position in Chicago.

Going from a small market like South Dakota to the number three market in the nation isn't very common. But there I was, making the move after just two and half years in the business. Saying *yes* to the opportunity was easy; what came after was a lot harder. It took me a few months to come through my initial transition, and I'm thankful my mom was with me for the first thirty days. She set up my apartment, made meals for me every day, and put a big stash of ready-made meals in the freezer for me before she left. This was our second relocation trip from state to state; my first move was from Los Angeles (where I lived for a short time) to Dallas (where many of my things were) to Sioux Falls. I had thought that move with help from both of my parents was rough, but my move to Chicago proved to be a lot more difficult. But in spite of it all, my mom and I worked well together to get things done.

## It All Comes Down to R.E.S.P.E.C.T.

We have learned that life constantly presents mothers and daughters with opportunities to either become bitter or better. We have also learned through our ups and downs that we both need to keep open minds and be willing to change and grow as new situations present themselves. This ongoing process has helped each of us in our own way to develop the ability to keep first things first—because the issues of life do come, and many times they come unexpectedly. Looking back on everything we have come through up to this point, we have come to the conclusion that it all comes down to R.E.S.P.E.C.T.:

**R elationship** – Loving, living, and building a strong foundation

**E steem** – Honoring each other and giving what's needed most

**S pirituality** – Putting God first

**P** **atience** – Expressing kindness and understanding, even when it hurts

**E** **xpectation** – Believing and releasing the best in every situation

**C** **ommunication** – Speaking the truth and hearing each other's hearts

**T** **reasuring** – Valuing each other first, in and through it all

## Building a Strong RELATIONSHIP

As a mother, I took on the role of taking the lead in building a healthy relationship with my daughter. The first thing that I learned, even while I was pregnant, is that becoming a parent involves sacrifice. At times, that was difficult for me because I had to consistently deny my own needs to do what was best for my child. I think it is best said that becoming a good parent takes willing sacrifice that comes from love. Although it's hard to admit, there were times over the years when I wasn't always as willing as I should have been and situations where I could have done better. But sacrifice is required, whether we're changing diapers, getting up for middle-of-the-night feedings, helping with homework, or going to school meetings and activities. A new level of sacrifice is required when we later come alongside our adult children to be of help and support while allowing them to stand on their own and make their own decisions. As we do all these things and more through the seasons of life, we build strong relationships with our children.

While our children grow and mature, there are countless opportunities for us to become bitter or better. When Sarah was a baby, she never wanted to take a nap, and she always wanted to be in the center of everything that was going on. I was tired and at times longed for breaks during those early years to have a little time for myself. So I gave my energetic little one the nickname "Marathon Sarah." But what's funny is that as she got older, Sarah became my hangout buddy, especially when I'd go places with my best friend Miralee. Years later, I realized that she had picked up a lot of things from being a marathon "hanger-outer."

Sarah matured quickly and has always had the gift of good common sense. She's a relationship person. And she always seems to be in the center of what's going on around her. I didn't see this clearly when she was a baby, and I wasn't always as aware of this as I should have been as she grew up, but I definitely see it now. Even her career bears witness of how strong she is in relationships.

* * * * * * * * * * *

At a young age, having a relationship with your parents isn't "the cool" thing to do. But my mother and I were different. Like she said, we were close even when I was young. She was always doing something adventurous. From white water rafting to mountain climbing, she did it all, and I was right behind her. But the dynamic of our relationship changed when I graduated from high school. I remember sitting down with her one day and having a heart-to-heart talk. Since I was staying home for a year and going to community college, I wanted to make sure we were both on the same page. I was starting to go out with friends and understood the importance of keeping your parents in the loop. I didn't want to sneak out to a club; I wanted my parents to know exactly where I was. Our conversation really took our relationship to the next level. It was the start of our "adult" relationship.

## Expressing ESTEEM

We've all heard the saying, "Honor your mother and father." This is something I have tried to do all my life. But there are several situations where my mother has honored me. Time and time again, she loves me beyond my mistakes and trusts my decisions. In 2010, I graduated from college and started looking for my first television job. I had gotten a lot of hands-on experience in college as the news director for our station and had done two great internships at BET and the leading news station in Dallas. So I thought that I would get a job fast, but that wasn't the case.

After tons of applications and a few failed interviews, I was a college grad with no job. Instead of staying home to continue looking for a job, I moved to Los Angeles. This wasn't something that was planned either. I literally decided to move one day, and a week later, I was gone. That wasn't like me, but I needed a change. Instead of arguing with me or trying to get me to stay, my parents supported me. My mother even kept my puppy which at that time wasn't house trained. She honored me and gave me what I needed at that time, and I couldn't be more grateful.

* * * * * * * * * * *

When I think of expressing esteem from a mother's perspective, it takes me back to something special Sarah did for her father and me when she graduated from high school. She presented us with a beautiful plaque that read: "To Mom and Dad. So many times the appreciation I have for you goes unspoken. I'd just like to take this time to thank you for all the encouragement, guidance, and understanding you have shown me throughout my years. You've always been there when I have needed you. Love, Sarah."

At that time, although I felt that I had done everything I could to be there for both of my children as often as I could, I didn't feel worthy of receiving her kind words. I had a very busy job and consistently worked well over forty hours a week. Added to this were a flurry of church activities and other family and personal responsibilities. As a result, while I was there to take care of things at home, I wasn't able to be at home as much as I wanted to or be more present at school activities. I constantly felt guilty about it. But regardless, Sarah honored me and her father for what we had done in her life. That's what I call esteem. Even now, Sarah continues to show esteem for me. And often, like she did so well during our trip from Sioux Falls to Chicago, she expresses it in the little things.

## Growing in SPIRITUALITY

All my life, my mother has been my spiritual beacon. Even when I wasn't where I was supposed to be spiritually, I knew her prayers were keeping me out of certain situations. When I began to actively seek the Lord in my early twenties, she had a wealth of information that helped me to further my relationship with Him. I really began to see how important this was while I was living in Sioux Falls. I was the closest I have ever been to the Lord and was seeing Him move in my life like never before. At that time, my best friends who were my age weren't in the same place in their lives, so my mom was the only person who was close to me that could really relate to my situation. This opened a new door for our relationship and opened me up to a deeper relationship with God.

\* \* \* \* \* \* \* \* \* \* \*

It amazes me to think about how different it has been for my children spiritually than it was for me growing up. Unlike

Sarah and her brother Asa, I didn't grow up in church. After going to church off and on in my childhood, I got saved when I was a teenager, but I didn't have a real one-to-one encounter with the Lord and give my heart to Him completely until (like Sarah) I was in my early twenties. When I truly met Jesus and He became real to me, it changed my life. I fell radically in love with Him and began to live my life to please Him in every way I knew how.

Looking back, my husband Kim and I had only the best intentions for our children by taking them to church regularly, most of the time twice a week. And spiritually speaking, it is true that when we "train up" our children in the way they should go, they won't depart from it when they are old (Proverbs 22:6). But I have to admit that we probably could have been more balanced in some areas.

Let me clarify. I believe our spiritual life—our relationship with God—is our highest priority. But as a mother, I could have been monitoring my children's progress more closely. I was extremely busy with my work and commitments at church, assuming that Sarah and Asa were as connected as my husband and I were, but Sarah later told me that she wasn't. She didn't relate to many of the kids at our church, and when she later had an experience with the Holy Spirit there, instead of being excited, she was so afraid that she was crying. Needless to say, that was a wake-up call for me.

Now I understand that true spirituality is expressed first in our relationship with God, which then flows to our relationships with our spouse, children, and extended family members. Then from the authenticity of these relationships, true spiritual life can be released in and through us at church, in ministry, among our friends and coworkers, and finally, to other people we meet. I have learned that sometimes the most spiritual thing we can do is simply be there to listen, comfort, and give practical advice. It has taken me years to learn this lesson . . . and can I tell you that I'm still in the process of learning? Amen.

## Practicing PATIENCE

One of my most difficult experiences learning patience as a mother took place when Sarah was in college. One night the Lord gave me a dream about Sarah that revealed she was sick and weak. It was so real that I called her the next morning and asked her how she had been feeling. She was more than surprised. She hadn't been feeling well, and being "grown," she didn't want to talk me about it. But when she opened up, that's when my ability to be patient was put to the test.

I can only say that God moved powerfully in that situation. We went before Him together, addressed the issue, and He moved. Needless to say, we are far beyond that now. But there's one thing I'll never forget. In that dream, Jesus was carrying my daughter. As I watched Him with Sarah, I could feel how much He loved her. That stayed in the forefront of my mind then, and it remains to this day.

To practice patience as we bear with our children, we need to empty ourselves of self and operate from the foundation of love. At times, tough love is necessary. Other times, tenderness is key. But at all times, we need to demonstrate our love, not anger, bitterness, or judgmentalism. Love conquers all.

\* \* \* \* \* \* \* \* \* \* \*

Patience is key in any relationship. For my mom and I, there have been a few circumstances when I learned about patience. The first thing that comes to mind is a period when my parents were going through a few things in their relationship. I guess you could say what happened was on the serious side, and it was also the first time I knew more about things they were going through. When I was younger, my parents didn't confide in me; but as I grew older, they both began to open up. This was great, but it was also challenging at times because I had to remain unbiased. In that situation, my mom confided something to me that was very sensitive; and at first, only I knew about it, and I couldn't say anything until some things played out. Thankfully, they ended up working through the issue, and it brought the three of us closer together, but it definitely required patience on my part.

## Believing with EXPECTATION

It can be difficult to believe and release the best in every situation, especially as a parent. Having gone through different situations with our children, we can sometimes fall into the trap of not expecting them to get beyond their immaturity, weaknesses, and at times, bad decisions. But Galatians 6:7b (Amplified Bible) says, "For whatever a man sows, that and that only is what he will reap."[1] [[REF]] In context, this verse speaks to sowing to our "flesh" (our lower nature) and reaping decay, ruin, and destruction versus sowing to the Spirit and reaping eternal life (v. 8). But this principle also holds true in how we relate to our children. If we show them that we expect them to succeed, we are planting seeds to produce that result. And if we act like we expect them to fail or make them feel as though we have no expectations of them at all, we are sowing seeds for the opposite to happen.

In the situation with Sarah that I mentioned in the last section, I had to pray and trust God to help me say and do what was right in His eyes and best for my daughter. And He did. Not only was the situation quickly resolved, but Sarah and I and her best friend Marcia also ended up at the altar together one day where I was attending Bible classes. In that place, God caused each of us to sow to the Spirit, and then He did what only He could do . . . and the proof is in the pudding. The things that have unfolded in Sarah's life since that time are expectation fulfilled, the incredible blessing of the Lord.

\* \* \* \* \* \* \* \* \* \* \*

Speaking of expectation, this chapter is the first time my mother and I have worked together on a book. We both had our own expectations, but the path to reach those expectations and finish has been tough. Since joining this project, I have moved, struggled with computer issues, been asked to work extra shifts at work, and was really sick. All these things topped off an already challenging schedule. I am one of the producers for *Good Day Chicago* on Fox 32, and in order to have the morning show ready and written, I have to come in the night before. Yes, I work the dreaded second "graveyard" shift. My schedule has made collaborating with my mother difficult. But the fact that you're reading this now is proof that we pulled through. Despite the obstacles I faced, she believed in me and encouraged me to keep pressing on. Her expectation in me, like during the situation she mentioned when I was in college, helped me through every sentence and every paragraph.

## Developing Healthy COMMUNICATION

If you truly knew me, you'd know that I wear my heart on my sleeve. I say what I mean, even when it's tough. I'm a communicator at my core, and I cherish my relationships. It can be challenging at times to always be completely honest with your parents, not because you don't want to but for fear of being judged or that they won't love you because of your mistakes.

Communicating with my mom and dad has been something I've had to work through. But I have always opted for being forthcoming and truthful. In my relationship with my mom, talking openly has really paid off. Communicating with her gives me a different perspective than what my friends may say. And God gave me a mother who, despite her own feelings, loves me through my faults. This unconditional love has allowed me to let her in and allow her to be an example to me. By being open with her, I've received wisdom beyond my years.

\* \* \* \* \* \* \* \* \* \* \*

Being the mother of a born communicator, I have to say that the Lord has truly processed me in saying what I think. Hearing what Sarah (or anyone else) thought was generally less challenging for me because I learned to suppress what I said from an early age. So by default, I became a good listener. But from the time Sarah could put two or three words together, she was expressing herself, even telling on herself when she had done something wrong. That always tickled me. So much so that when I had to discipline her for doing whatever she'd done, I'd often struggle to keep a straight look on my face and keep from laughing.

As Sarah grew up through elementary school age into her teen years, it was more difficult at times to hear what she thought—because for Sarah, she simply says what's on her mind. My challenge was to respond to her instead of reacting. As a parent, I had to learn how to maintain my role as her mother while at the same time showing her my humanity, sometimes even sharing from my mistakes, so that she could better understand and work through her situations.

Although neither Sarah nor I have always hit the bull's-eye when it comes to communication, we have definitely grown in this area. More often than not, we can express ourselves openly, honestly, and positively. And when we run into snags, we can revisit where we went wrong and talk things out. Each time we do, we're stronger for it.

## Living by TREASURING

From the time she was born, Sarah has been a priceless treasure to me. So has her brother Asa. But I'll say again that through the seasons of our lives, there were times when I felt that I could have done a better job demonstrating my love. But more importantly, I am doing my best to learn from my mistakes and let them both know—regularly and in practical ways—how much they mean to me. You see, treasuring someone goes beyond words. It means that we give them our love, our time, our understanding, and our prayers. We put their needs above our own. We stand behind them and give them support, even when they make mistakes. We listen to them. We encourage them. We confront them when it's necessary. We do anything we can to be there for them when they need a helping hand.

I thank God that throughout our lives and through many ups and downs, He has graciously allowed Sarah and me to learn how to treasure each other in new ways. Now in my "seasoned" years, I am grateful to call her my precious best friend. Like she did during our trip from Sioux Falls to Chicago, Sarah consistently warms my heart by showing me the special place I hold in hers. Often when I think of Sarah (and her brother too), I remember the promise in Exodus 20:12 and thank God for this blessing: "Honor your father and your mother, that your days may be long in the land that the Lord your God is giving you" (ESV).[2] [[REF]]

\* \* \* \* \* \* \* \* \* \* \*

I have treasured my mother since day one. I remember as a little girl looking up to her as she juggled a full-time job and full-time college classes, thinking how smart and beautiful she was with her long curly hair and her glasses sitting at the tip of her nose. I wanted to be like her. I wanted to make her proud. My mother is my best friend, and I'm not sure where I would be without her guidance. Our relationship has truly been a driving force in my life. And now I understand it is because we always chose to be better, not bitter—because as we talked about before writing this chapter, we've learned how to R.E.S.P.E.C.T. each other as mother, daughter, and the closest of friends. The relationship we have built is unbreakable.

## Measure Your R.E.S.P.E.C.T.

So what about you? How do you measure your R.E.S.P.E.C.T. with your daughter or mother? Take a few minutes to really think about and respond to the following questions. Then we encourage you to do whatever it takes as you work through your own challenges, not to become bitter but to get better and better.

1.  Do you and your mother or daughter have a strong relationship? Have you esteemed each other the way you really want to? If not, how can you change to make things better?
2.  How has spirituality come into play in your relationship? Do you put God first, or is this a difficult area for you? Either way, make this a matter of prayer, and let God help you to grow, individually and together.

3. As mother and daughter, how have you developed in patience, expectation, and communication? Think of times when you've had breakthroughs in these areas. Then talk it over and take time to celebrate each one.
4. How well do you demonstrate your love? Write a note to your mom or daughter, saying how much you treasure her and thanking her, in spite of your challenges, for the ways she treasures you.

End Notes

[1] The *Amplified Bible*, WORDsearch® Bible 10. Powered by LifeWay. Build 10.6.0.81. All rights reserved.
[2] The *English Standard Version*, WORDsearch® Bible 10. Powered by LifeWay. Build 10.6.0.81. All rights reserved.

Dr. Stan (Breakthrough) Harris and
son Staff Sgt. Joshua Harris

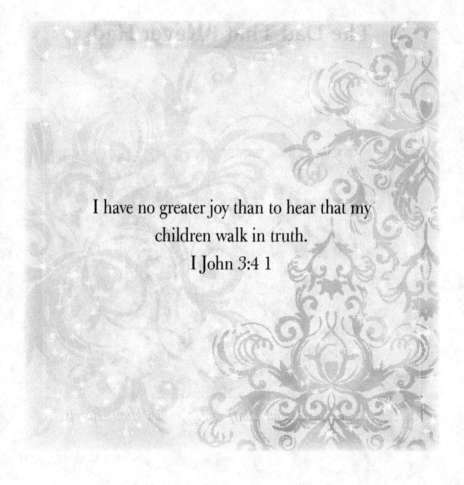

I have no greater joy than to hear that my
children walk in truth.
I John 3:4 1

# The Dad That I Never Had

*Dr Stan Harris and Staff Sgt. Joshua Stan Harris*

$\mathcal{S}$ ome people think that they can't shine or reach their potential because they never had a star in their life, a role model, in my case a Dad. But before I get too deep into this, let me let you read the written version of a voicemail I received July 3rd 2011. "Hey Dad it's Josh, no need for you to call me back and actually it's better that this goes on voicemail in case you want to ever play it back." (Little did he know almost 4 years later, I'm playing or writing this for a book, that we get to write this chapter together) "I don't think I've ever thanked you for this, but thanks for being the Father you never had." "Most guys in general learn from a role model and it's very hard to learn without an example." "I appreciate the fact that you are always there for me, and how you have made a smooth transition from being my Dad to also becoming my close friend, if not my best friend." "I enjoy your company, and every time I go on a road trip, you're the first person that I call because more than likely you will answer and talk to me for however long it takes to make sure I stay awake." "I want you to know how much I appreciate you and please know the things you do for me are not taken for granted." "Have a happy July 4th weekend, I love you very much, and will see you soon, bye."

Now this voicemail has been played by me over and over again many times, but the first time I heard it, I actually cried out of joy! Here's why, Joshua never knew this, but I made a promise to myself that I would one day be "the Dad that I never had." Now some 40 years later my oldest son verbalizes to me what I had verbalized to my Heavenly Father! You see my Dad left when I was three years of age and I never heard from him through the years. I longed for a visit, even a phone call, actually I would have even settled for a letter. (This was a long time before emails) He never sent my Mom a dime to help raise the three of us boys, though now it's 5 boys.

Growing up in the Ghetto was hard enough, but there is something in a little boy, especially an alpha boy that wants the approval of his Dad. It really hurt when my favorite Television show came on in the 1970's called "The Courtship Of Eddies Father" which was the story of a little boy (Brandon Cruz) being raised by his Dad (Bill Bixby) who was a widower. (*The Courtship of Eddie's Father* is an American television sitcom based on the 1963 movie of the same name, which was based on the book written by Mark Toby (edited by Dorothy Wilson). It tells the story of a widower, Tom Corbett (played by Bill Bixby), who is a magazine publisher, and his son, Eddie (played by Brandon Cruz), who believes his father should marry, and manipulates situations surrounding the women his father is interested in. ABC had acquired the rights to the story; the series debuted on September 17, 1969, and was last broadcast on March 1, 1972.)est Friend", by Harry Nilsson

The theme song by HARRY NILSSON
**People let me tell you 'bout my best friend,**
**He's a warm hearted person who'll love me till the end.**
**People let me tell you 'bout my best friend,**
**He's a one boy cuddly toy, my up, my down, my pride and joy.**

**People let me tell you 'bout him he's so much fun**
**Whether we're talkin' man to man or whether we're**
**talking son to son.**
**Cause he's my best friend.**
**Yes he's my best friend.**

Wow, I still hear that song now, and I remember crying as a little boy watching the TV as they would play ball together, throw a Frisbee or walk on the beach. I hungered to have that kind of relationship. At times we would move in with my Grandparents, but even then my Grandfather was an alcoholic and I would have to drag him out of the bars, at my Grandmothers request. They called him "Happy" because he was drunk quite a bit, so needless to say we never had any conversations or had a change to play ball etc.

But I want you to know that I had an Uncle (Bobby Stewart) although a womanizer, and ruff character, (The police raided his house and found 11 guns), he would take me with him from time to time to do odd jobs. Wow, I loved the time working with Unc (short for Uncle) even though he fussed at me constantly, he would pay me thus I would go buy some candy. Now you talk about feeling good, there is no better feeling for a child than to be with an adult whom he can watch and learn things from.

So I want to give you a few tips that helped me turn my situation from what could have been terrible to a wonderful relationship with my own son/sons.

Tip #1. Pain and adversity causes some to break yet causes others to break records. So why not decide to do, or be better because of your pain. One of my quotes that people love to hear the most when I'm speaking at an event is, "Within your pain, is hidden power." Behind the glory there's always a story so the old adage, "no pain, no gain" could be changed to, "much pain can lead to much gain." Every powerful person I know or story I've heard was born out of hurt, pain and struggle. Diamonds are simple pieces of coal that responded extremely well to the pressure. The long agitation experienced from a piece of sand in an Oyster becomes a beautiful expensive Pearl! So don't let hurt... hurt you, but rather help you!

Tip #2. Every asset has a liability and every liability has a corresponding asset! The show I loved portrayed a son having a great relationship with his Dad, but his mother had died! As a matter of fact Eddie was always trying to set his Dad up with a wife, why, because although he had an awesome Dad, he missed his Mom and wanted a replacement. Now my Dad was gone, but at least my Mom wasn't dead! And my Mom and I had an awesome relationship until her death in 1990. There's an up for every down, and a darkness before the dawn. The liabilities are the negatives and the assets are the positives, but a battery cannot work with two positives. Some people complain about cold of Winter and the heat of Summer while others enjoy each season for what it brings!

Tip #3. Don't allow what you can't do to keep you from what you can do. Don't allow what you don't have to keep you from appreciating what you do have. So what I'm saying is, I couldn't change my Dad not being around but I could make sure that I spent time with my son's when they came along! You see some people get so focused on what they don't have that they loose site of what they do have. As a matter of face once I grew up and got married, we had 4 beautiful children, (a beautiful girl and 3 boy's) and I took my children all over the World with me as I would travel and preach in Churches, do Karate Demonstrations and speak for Businesses. We have wrestled, boxed, done Karate, played football, basketball, jumped on a trampoline etc. I think not having a Dad made me sensitive in areas that I may not have been and of course by no means have I been a perfect Dad, I have been a Dad who is being perfected!

Tip #4. Just make up your mind, and do like you decided! There is something powerful about the mind. "When I make up my mind to do something, God orchestrates circumstances to align themselves in my favor, when I say 'I can't', my mind stops trying, but when I ask 'How can I?', my mind keeps searching until it finds a way. There is a way and I will find it, and if not I will invent it." The power of the mind is so underestimated, it's an untapped power that needs to be harnessed. You have more power than you know! (Prov 23:7 For as he thinketh in his heart, so is he.)

Tip #5. Speak about what you want instead of what you don't want! So many people forget that what you focus on or talk about the longest becomes the strongest. People are quick to tell you what they don't want, but almost stutter when asked, "what do you want?" When you get very clear and focused on what you want and learn to say it, (Job 22:28 Thou shalt also decree a thing, and it shall be established unto thee), (Prov 18:21 Death and life are in the power of the tongue) then you can start producing it just as I did although it's been a 40 year process!

Tip #6 Do things in spite of. Now what I mean is learn to give your Son's compliments in spite of the fact that you never received them. Give them your blessing/approval though you never received it from your Father. Give them an example in spite of the fact that you didn't have one.

Now I want you to hear a few pointers from my oldest Son Joshua who is a Staff Sargent with the Marines. Joshua is a true gentleman, a warrior, a man of high integrity! He is handsome, smart, spiritual, and a meek man. By the way meekness is not weakness but rather strength under control, and Joshua demonstrates this unlike anyone else I know. He is one of the most amazing spoken word artists that I have ever heard and he even got to speak at a meeting along with myself and Les Brown. He has become an amazing man and I'm honored to have him give you a few tips on Father /Son relationships. "Ok Josh, take it away son. "Originally, my dad and I were each to write a chapter, but it was later learned that there was an expectation of a chapter speaking about father and son relationships. From that expectation this was made. My dad wrote his part in a day or two, and I followed suit two days later. This isn't planned, this isn't rehearsed, this was barely talked out…it's just an understanding of what it means to be a man and our own personal experiences on the subject. One of my dad's recommendations was that I write five tips from the standpoint of a son (who had a father) and Staff Sergeant of Marines about what it means to be a man and what might be helpful for fathers and sons to focus on. I would like to add, while writing this, that these pointers aren't gender specific nor are they in any particular order, since it would be very difficult to rate these in an "order" of importance.

1. Responsibility (respond with ability), reliability, and living up to your word: I think one of the most underrated characteristics of being a good human being in general is just living up to your word. I think a lot of this has to do with making a way instead of making excuses (we'll get to that later). I think it helps to think of your word as iron. If you say it, mean it and treat it like a promise. If you say it and you didn't mean it like a promise, still follow through if someone calls you out on it. Not only will this be extremely helpful as a parent (consistency and reliability is very important for people who otherwise have little to no control over their own lives), but it will make you an invaluable employee. You don't show up whenever you want to, you show up on time. You don't do whatever you want to, you do what you're supposed to. Bottom line: it won't always be fun, but it will greatly impress those around you and make you a person who is respected and sought after. You may get a lot of "will you take me to work in the morning," "call me for work in the morning," or "be my gym partner/hold me accountable" but that's not always a bad thing, and if the situation is reversed your friends are more likely to return the favor.

2. Value people over things: exactly what it says. This is going to be a short one: if they don't respect your things and what you ask of them, perhaps they don't need to be in your life. However, nothing that you own is worth the life of another human being (and it really shouldn't be valued over your own freedom). This includes everything from Jordans, to a suit, to a vehicle. Things can be replaced, lives cannot. Once upon a time you were probably someone else's knucklehead (or maybe you still are), try to remember that and be the compassion that person may need.

3. Be respectable (clothes, demeanor, language, tattoos): being respectable is really a complete concept. Being respectable is more than just how you dress, how you carry yourself, or even how you speak. Being respectable sometimes means demanding the respect that you deserve from others. This doesn't have to be rude or confrontational, but letting someone know that you don't appreciate or don't deserve negative treatment may well be all that is needed. I have had to many times stand up for my decision to be a vegetarian in my earlier years (it honestly didn't start out as my own choice), my decision to stay a virgin into my twenties, and the fact that I am almost always seen with a book on my person. It's ok to stand up to someone and ask them what is so bad about a responsible life choice that has healthy, educational, or moral benefits. As a side note, please be aware of what you are tattooing on your body and where you are placing it. I love tattoos and while most people would consider me to have four tattoos, they cover most of my back, most of my pecs, one forearm, and a shoulder. I have huge tattoos. The thing that the Marine Corps

taught me (after I got my forearm tattoo) is that they shouldn't be visible in professional clothing. Tattoos are your choice, but hiring is an employer's.

4.  Respect other people (especially all women): while you are demanding the respect that you have earned, please remember to respect others. That includes the old man, the racist, the gay man, the person who thinks pets are children, and most especially all women. The world would be a very different place is we as men treated all women like our own mothers, sisters, daughters, cherished female in our lives, or how we would want our own daughters, nieces, or godchildren treated. On the flip side, this also applies to women. If someone doesn't fit into your idea of what it means to be womanly or manly, it is not ok to make their lives harder. It is entirely ok to help them if they are willing to accept it, and pray for them either way. God teaches love and to leave the judging to Him. That doesn't mean that you can't stand up for what you believe in or that they have to be your best friend. It means that sometimes you have to just walk away and leave people to God. Men, please remember to treat a woman (and your own body) the way you want the woman that you will one day marry to be. If you want her to be free of emotional baggage, don't cheat on the one that you are with. If you don't want her to have slept around with a lot of men, then don't sleep around yourself. Be what you expect out of others and what you look for. As Lyfe Jennings said "don't be a nickel out here looking for a dime." I think the comedian Reginald D. Hunter said it best, though "Many of us are not qualified for our own dreams." If you're wondering why you keep ending up with terrible

people: perhaps that's who you're attracting (change your standards), perhaps that's just what you're settling for (raise your standards), and pray that it's not the only people that you qualify for (change your actions). Remember this: if you expect others to play by your rules, you're going to be disappointed. That works for understanding how to interact with people in general, however you can still hold out for that one that does.

5. Hard work not excuses: the bottom line is that too many of us think that we are owed something. Guess what? That is absolutely not true. Life is not fair, no one is looking to give you a thing, and honestly not many people (if any) truly care about your feelings and if you succeed or fail. That sounds very harsh and it is. However, it is also the truth. We understand that certain people have physical and mental handicaps, but for those that don't it's just that much harder to accept their many excuses for not having a job, not being on time, or whatever else. No one is perfect, and there are times that you're going to have to own up to failing, but commit to do better next time. It's not the fault of traffic that you're late, it's your fault and you'll make up the time tomorrow, or just start heading out earlier if you have to in order to make sure that you make it on time. The circumstances change, but the concept doesn't. You make a way for things that you care about. You make excuses for those things that you don't care about. Think about how many couch cushions you may have tossed looking for change, perhaps scoured the entire house, to get that cheeseburger or fry that you wanted. Do you put that same effort into applying for a job? My last point on this is one that I taught my junior Marines: you haven't tried to the best of your abilities

until you've tried to the best of the abilities of everyone around you. Pool your resources, don't be afraid to ask questions or seek help. We succeed as a species through team work. Read about the tower of Babel, or try to figure out how ancient Egyptians constructed the pyramids. Now, imagine what would have gotten done if you had been in charge of construction. So I trust these simple steps and pointers will help you as they have helped my Dad and I.

# Sponsors

# IS YOUR FAMILY COVERED?

In light of the school shootings, 9/11, and Hurricane Katrina, just to name a few.
Is your family prepared for an emergency?

## DO YOU:

- Have a Living Will?
- Need to update the one you have?
- Need a contract reviewed?
- Need your child support increased?
- Need help with a traffic ticket?
- Need help with a legal issue?

## HAVE YOU:

- Pre-planned your final wishes?
- Made plans for your children if something happens to you?

## PROTECT YOUR FAMILY
Get Your Living Will Today for only $29.95

## FOR INFORMATION
Check out my website at: www.legalshieldassociate.com/go/teresahailey
Email me at - teresahailey@yahoo.com
Listen to our information line at 512-703-6148 option #2

173

Printed in the United States
By Bookmasters